Kingdom Manifesto

Wycliffe Studies in Gospel, Church, and Culture

GENERAL EDITOR: THOMAS P. POWER

The series entitled Wycliffe College Studies in Gospel, Church, and Culture is intended to present topical subject matter in an accessible form and seeks to appeal to a broad audience. Typically titles in the series derive from sermons given by the faculty of Wycliffe College, Toronto, in its Founders' Chapel. The current volume on Ezekiel is the eighth in the series.

Kingdom Manifesto

*Meditations on the
Gospel of Matthew*

EDITED BY
Jason N. Yuh

WIPF *&* STOCK · Eugene, Oregon

KINGDOM MANIFESTO
Meditations on the Gospel of Matthew

Wipf & Stock
An Imprint of Wipf and Stock Publishers
199 W. 8th Ave., Suite 3
Eugene, OR 97401

www.wipfandstock.com

PAPERBACK ISBN: 978-1-6667-1460-9
HARDCOVER ISBN: 978-1-6667-1461-6
EBOOK ISBN: 978-1-6667-1462-3

07/30/21

Contents

List of Contributors

Stephen Andrews, Principal, Wycliffe College

Stephen Chester, Professor of New Testament, Wycliffe College

Ann Jervis, Professor of New Testament, Wycliffe College

Peter Mason, Emeritus Principal, Wycliffe College

Judy Paulsen, Professor of Evangelism, Wycliffe College

Thomas Power, Adjunct Professor of Church History, Wycliffe College

Ephraim Radner, Professor of Historical Theology, Wycliffe College

Catherine Sider-Hamilton, Professor of New Testament, Wycliffe College

Glen Taylor, Emeritus Professor of Old Testament, Wycliffe College

Jason N. Yuh, Ph.D. Candidate in New Testament, Wycliffe College

Introduction

JASON N. YUH

WHAT EXACTLY IS THE Gospel of Matthew?

There are many complex ways of answering this rather simple question. Scholars might broach the debate about the genre of Matthew. Is it a form of ancient biography? What kind of historical value does it contain? Or perhaps they would attempt to reconstruct the cultural milieu of the text and hypothesize on the social factors that led to its production.

Christians might view the text as a set of moral teachings that they ought to practice. They certainly recognize that the focal point of the Gospel is Jesus, but in practice, their focus is on themselves: are *their* lives resembling the qualities of Jesus? How are *their* lives enhanced through their knowledge of him?

Those outside of academic and Christian circles might not think much of the Gospel at all. Its origins, historicity, and value are all dubious, some might think. The text is a démodé document that has survived merely through political propaganda. Therefore, the Gospel should have no meaningful impact in our modern setting.

Even a cursory read of the Gospel of Matthew makes clear that it is concerned with the identity of Jesus Christ. The Gospel begins with a genealogy that implies Jesus' continuation and fulfillment of the Old Testament, or Hebrew Bible, and it ends with his very last words, which exhort his followers to have everyone live in submission to him and which remind them that he will always be with them (Matt 28:18–20). The book seeks to answer questions that center around him: what was *his* purpose? What did *he* do? Why was *his* life significant?

I am eager to introduce the following meditations, because they assume the true answer to the simple question posed above. These meditations attempt not to focus on tangential topics that relate to Jesus, even though these are important. Rather, they seek to focus simply on who Jesus is. Because the year 2020 has exposed the fragility, corruption, and misery of humanity, such a focus is not only welcome but sorely needed. Humanity does not merely require self-help books that provide practical steps for improvement or philosophical musings that explain away suffering. Humanity is in dire need of something outside of itself: a Savior. The authors of these chapters are soberly aware of this truth, and they resist the temptation to reduce Jesus to a miracle worker who provides temporary relief or a commendable example that is to be imitated. Instead, in their own distinctive ways, they affirm the bold and ever-urgent proclamation that Jesus is the Savior of all people—Jews and gentiles, the poor and the rich, scholars and the uneducated, and those inside and outside the church.

1

What Shall I Bring Him?

STEPHEN CHESTER

IN BOTH MATTHEW'S GOSPEL and Luke's Gospel, there are surprising characters who crop up in the stories of the birth of Jesus. In Luke, the surprising characters are the shepherds. The first announcement of Christ's birth is given to people who are regarded as the lowest of the low within Israel. It is poor and marginalized workers who are witnesses of the joy of heaven in the form of the heavenly choir and who are the first to visit the newborn child. The last are made first in the kingdom of God. As we think about the wise men, we could easily continue with the same theme. True, these individuals are not poor or uneducated like the shepherds, but they are still very odd choices as witnesses to the birth of Israel's Messiah. The word "magi," with which they are labeled in Matthew's Gospel, is not one that is used positively elsewhere in the Bible. Daniel 2:12 names as magi the "magicians, enchanters, sorcerers, and astrologers" (2:2 NIV) who are not able to interpret the dream of their master, King Nebuchadnezzar of Babylon. God reveals the meaning not to them but to his true servant Daniel.[1] In the New Testament, the only other magus who appears is Elymas, the attendant of Sergius Paulus, the Roman proconsul of Cyprus, who opposes the gospel and who is struck blind by Paul (Acts 13:4–12). To be a magus is not a good thing. Even if one has considerable knowledge, it is godless, false knowledge. It is the kind of learning of which the people of God are to steer clear. Yet, as Isaiah 60 foretells, God chooses and uses these mysterious gentile visitors. They are outsiders, people who might be expected not to understand and not to take seriously the granting of a Messiah to Israel. Yet, they are found worshipping the infant Jesus, and their doing so foreshadows the revelation that will come to the gentiles after Christ's death and resurrection, when the gospel will be preached to all. The truth about Jesus will be for the gentiles also, and the wise men are the very first people to be part of that. God is truly the God of the Jewish people, and yet, through Christ the gentiles will also be admitted to God's people.

However, there is another aspect of the story of the wise men that is also very important. They are the ones who worship the infant Jesus; they are the ones who bring him gifts. When we think of the wise men, we think of gifts and the whole process of giving that is such a big focus of our own customs and practices in the Christmas season. Of course, in bringing their gifts the wise men are not initiating something new. They are not the first to give a gift. Instead, they are reciprocating, for God has already given the greatest gift of all. As the prophet Isaiah puts it, "For a child has been born for us, / a son given to us; authority rests upon his shoulders; / and he is named / Wonderful

1. Unless otherwise noted, all Scripture quotations in this chapter are from the NRSV.

Counselor, Mighty God, / Everlasting Father, Prince of Peace" (Isa 9:6). The gift is Jesus himself, and even if the wise men do not fully understand what they are doing, they are responding to God's gift by bringing gifts of their own before Jesus. The wise men are enabled to respond appropriately to who Jesus is. Even though they expect a palace and are instead led to a humble dwelling, they still recognize that this baby is the king given by God, and they bring their own gifts in worship of him. Therefore, the other theme that the story of the wise men places before us is that of giving back to God. In Jesus, God has given us everything, even his own Son. Accordingly, we ought to give back. What will you give back to God? Now, that's a trickier question than it sounds at first blush. The wise men could bring gifts directly to Jesus here on earth, but Jesus is now seated at the right hand of the Father. We cannot go to Bethlehem and find the baby like they did. As the psalmist puts it, "The earth is the Lord's and all that is in it, / the world, and those who live in it" (Ps 24:1). Giving back to God is similar to trying to find the perfect gift for the person who has everything. While we know that for a variety of reasons it is truly important that we offer our gifts of money in church each week, none of us actually thinks that the God we worship is short of cash. God is not in need of a handout from us. Gift giving is a metaphor from human social practice that helps us genuinely understand our relationship with God, so there are ways in which giving back to God is like giving to another human being. However, there are also ways in which giving back to God and giving in God's kingdom are quite different from giving to another human being.

One of the ways in which Jesus helped people to think about God's upside-down kingdom and the ways in which it is different from human ways of thinking and behaving was by telling stories or parables. Thus, here is a parable-like story about giving back to God. It is actually a true story and not an imaginative fiction, and it contains a helpful perspective about the ways of God.

There was a young boy, only about four years old, whose aunt and uncle were misguided enough to buy him a harmonica for Christmas. It came with an instruction book on how to play the harmonica, but since the child was not yet old enough to read, his attempts to play the instrument were enthusiastic but completely tuneless. Now, the child's mother led the music in their local church, and one day the boy announced that he was going to play alongside her in the worship service. The mother did not know what to do. She did not want to reject the child's desire to participate in worship, but she was also anxious that people might be offended by his playing in a way that disrupted the service. She just hoped that the child would forget about what he had said, but of course, when Sunday came, he remembered. Her playing of the hymns was accompanied by her son blowing loudly on his harmonica. By the end of the service the mother was sure she was going to receive complaints, but something very different happened. Several older ladies in the congregation made a point of stopping by the piano on their way out of church. They told the boy how wonderful his playing had been, how much they had enjoyed hearing him play, and how much they were looking forward to hearing him play again the following week.

In this parable-like story, we see in a small way the character of God and the nature of his kingdom. We see, for instance, that there is joy and spontaneity in the way that the child offers the gift of his harmonica playing to

God. His playing may not be any good, but he offers it wholeheartedly, and it is beautiful for that reason. More importantly, the attitude of the older ladies in the story is instructive. They do not respond based on the quality of the child's musicianship. They understand what is happening, and they enjoy the playing not because of its quality but out of their affection for the child and their sense that despite all the wrong notes, this will be an acceptable offering in the eyes of God. The point is this: are not all our attempts to give back to God analogous to this story? It does not matter what we give; heaven has something better to offer. If, for tuneless harmonica playing, we were to substitute a perfect choral-symphonic performance of Bach's finest church music, the offering would still be feeble compared to what can be produced by the heavenly host. Yet, God's response is not to reject as inadequate our attempts to serve him. If our attempts are sincerely and wholeheartedly made, then God receives our gifts with joy.

This principle applies not only to our artistic efforts but also to our good deeds, to our faltering attempts to do what is right before God. About 450 years ago, John Calvin was preaching to a congregation in Geneva and trying to explain the same truth. Calvin says this:

> Picture a child who is seeking to obey his father: when his father asks him to do something, he will accept what the child does, even though the child may not understand what he is doing. The child may even break something in the process, and yet the father will not fret about the broken object when he sees his child's affection and willingness to obey. But if a man hires a servant, he will expect him to perform his task perfectly. Why? Because he is going to receive wages, and, therefore, he cannot afford to ruin what has

been committed to his hands. If the task is not done well, the master will not be content with it. Our Lord, speaking of the days of gospel grace, says that he will accept our service, just as a father accepts the obedience of his child, even if all that is done is of no value. That is to say, he does not accept it because it is perfect, for it is not, but he bears with us out of his abundant mercy. He shows himself to be so bountiful and kind to us by accepting what we do as if it were fully pleasing to him, although there is no inherent merit or worth in our works at all. Thus, we can have the freedom and the courage to serve God; we can know that God will bless all that we do for him because whatever is wrong with our offerings is washed away in the blood of the Lord Jesus Christ.[2]

What is striking about this illustration is how fresh it is even after all the years that have passed by since the sermon was preached. We are the children of God, and when we give wholeheartedly, sincerely, and with joy, this matters more than the quality of what is given. This illustration can easily be updated to speak in a contemporary way about who we are as children of God. All over the world, young children produce drawings and paintings that are presented to parents who keep them and display them, often, at least in Western contexts, on the refrigerator. Parents do not do this because they think they have the next Picasso or Rembrandt on their hands; very few of the pictures have any artistic merit whatsoever. They are precious to the parents because the person who made them is precious to them. This truth applies to all our giving back to God, for God is so far above us and his ways are so far

2. Calvin, *Sermons on the Epistle to the Galatians*, 202.

from our ways that anything we offer is more like the gift of a young child to a parent than it is like the gift of an adult to another adult. What we give is precious more because of *who* gives it than because of *what* is given.

When Martin Luther died, there was a scrap of paper in the room that had a few sentences written on it, the final of which was "We are beggars: this is true."[3] These were the last words the great Reformer ever wrote. They are enigmatic, but most scholars take them to refer to Luther's belief that whoever we are, we always come before God empty-handed, like a beggar. As Timothy George puts it, "We have no legs of our own on which to stand."[4] The truth is that in terms of what we might offer to God, we have nothing that he actually needs. Our gifts back to God are always like the tuneless playing of a harmonica, always like the broken object of which Calvin speaks, always like the sloppy painting fixed to the refrigerator. Hear the facts again: it is impossible for you or I or anyone else to bring to God any gift that he needs. *But* hear also the good news. There may be nothing we can bring as a gift that he needs, but God is like the older ladies in the parable-like story who welcome the child's harmonica playing. God is like the father of whom Calvin speaks, who does not mind that in the process of his child's obedience something gets broken. God is like the parent who joyfully receives and displays the painting of a young child. There is nothing you can give to God that he needs, but you do have exactly the gift that God most wants. The gift that God wants, all that the creator of the universe desires, is *you*. You and your life are the apple of God's eye, and you know that is true

3. Quoted in James M. Kittelson, *Luther the Reformer: The Story of the Man and His Career* (Minneapolis: Fortress Press, 1986, 2003), 297.

4. George, *Theology of the Reformers*, 105.

because God has given you the most precious gift he has, which is the life of his son. What God wants from you in return is simply that you give to him your own self. You: nothing more and nothing less.

The extraordinary thing is that if you give yourself to God, then although he does not need your time, your talents, or your money to accomplish his purposes in the world, these things will turn out to be strangely powerful when they are offered as part of the giving of yourself. By his grace, God will use your hands to do his work in the world. By his grace, yours will be the feet that are beautiful because they bring good news (Isa 52:7). By his grace, he will use you to serve your neighbor. By his grace, he will use you to set free the captives (Isa 61:1). By his grace, you will help to fight injustice. By his grace, you will bring comfort to those who mourn. By his grace, you will resist all the works of the evil one. And by his grace, you are baptized, and you are part of Christ's church, against which the gates of hell will not prevail (Matt 16:18). If I am making this sound like a question of our great and mighty deeds, then I am not saying it rightly. I am trying to talk not about what *we* will do, but about what *God* will do in us and through us. Furthermore, I am not talking about something different from the tuneless harmonica playing, the broken vessel, or the sloppy painting displayed on the refrigerator. I am talking about God taking and using precisely those things in all their weakness and inadequacy. Three times the apostle Paul prayed for God to take away a thorn in his flesh, but God said, "My grace is sufficient for you, for my power is made perfect in weakness."" Paul therefore said, "I will boast all the more gladly of my weaknesses, so that the power of Christ may dwell in me" (2 Cor 12:9).

Paul was talking about a physical infirmity, and I am talking about our moral deeds. The two things are not exactly parallel, but everything about our condition as fallen human beings partakes of weakness and inadequacy. Think even about the wise men. We do not usually think of them as inadequate and weak figures. They are rich, and they bring exotic gifts, but as explained previously, they are very odd servants for God to choose. They are not members of God's people, but are outsiders, and their learning is in the arts of superstition forbidden to Israel. Yet, the wise men are obedient to God, and by his grace God uses even their wretched astrology. They understand the significance of the star, and they make the journey when they might have decided it was just too difficult. They follow the light of the star, and they are led to the light of Christ. We have no way of knowing how many other magi noted the appearance of the star. Perhaps there were many, for the idea that the birth of great men was accompanied by phenomena in the night sky was common in the gentile world. The roads to Bethlehem, however, were not clogged with hordes of magi. This particular group travels, and in doing so, they make themselves available for God to use. Are you, and am I, available for God to use as they were? Are we, too, being led toward the light of Christ? The right question is not really what we should give to God, as if we have something that he needs. The right question is whether we are ready to give back to God the one thing that he truly desires, which is ourselves, and whether we are ready to be used by God to do his work in the world. The magi were ready when many in Israel were not. Are you? Am I? May God show us how it is that he wants to take our lives and use them. The ways in which God will use us will be many and varied, but they will always involve the willingness of a joyful heart. By God's grace, may we find that we do indeed have such joyful hearts as we hear again the story of God's love for us and of the indescribable gift of God's Son. Rejoice, for Christ is born of the Virgin Mary, and God is ready to receive willing hearts as the most precious offerings that could possibly be brought by those who worship the newborn king. Thanks be to God.

Scripture: Matt 2:1–12; Isa 60:1–6.

Questions:

1. In this meditation, the choice of the wise men as witnesses to the birth of Israel's Messiah is characterized as surprising. Is this how you are used to thinking about the figures of the wise men, or is this aspect surprising to you?

2. In what ways is God's gift of his Son, and our response to it, similar to our social practices of gift exchange, and in what ways are the two different from each other?

3. The meditation emphasizes that what God desires of us is that we respond to his gift of Jesus by giving ourselves. Nevertheless, that gift of our own selves must find concrete form. What are some appropriate ways in which it can be expressed?

2

Why Did God Allow Satan to Tempt Jesus?

GLEN TAYLOR

HAVE YOU EVER BEEN tempted to do something you knew you should not do? Your answer is almost certainly "Yes." Most of us can easily recall at least one challenging time, whether it was the temptation to steal something or to make a false statement for personal gain.

That was an easy question, so let me try asking another before embarking upon the much more difficult question reflected in the title of this essay. Why does God allow *us* to be tempted? Chances are, you will need to pause and think before answering, and for good reason. After a while you might say that in some cases, it is God's way of accomplishing some greater good, such as strengthening our character. And if you were to say that, you would be right; note, for example, what is said in Deuteronomy 8, which I quote at length because it forms an important backdrop to the story of Jesus' temptation. Note especially the three italicized segments.

> The whole commandment that I command you today you shall be careful to do, that you may

live and multiply, and go in and possess the land that the Lord swore to give to your fathers. And you shall remember the whole way that the Lord your God has led you these forty years in the wilderness, *that he might humble you, testing you to know what was in your heart, whether you would keep his commandments or not.* And he humbled you and let you hunger and fed you with manna, which you did not know, nor did your fathers know, that he might make you know that man does not live by bread alone, but man lives by every word that comes from the mouth of the Lord.[1] Your clothing did not wear out on you and your foot did not swell these forty years. Know then in your heart that, *as a man disciplines his son, the Lord your God disciplines you.* So you shall keep the commandments of the Lord your God by walking in his ways and by fearing him. For the Lord your God is bringing you into a good land, a land of brooks of water, of fountains and springs, flowing out in the valleys and hills, a land of wheat and barley, of vines and fig trees and pomegranates, a land of olive trees and honey, a land in which you will eat bread without scarcity, in which you will lack nothing, a land whose stones are iron, and out of whose hills you can dig copper. And you shall eat and be full, and you shall bless the Lord your God for the good land he has given you.

Take care lest you forget the Lord your God by not keeping his commandments and his rules and his statutes, which I command you today, lest, when you have eaten and are full and have built good houses and live in them, and when

---

1. The translation of the Jewish Publication Society Tanakh version plausibly clarifies the meaning as "that man may live on anything that the Lord decrees" (NJPS).

> your herds and flocks multiply and your silver
> and gold is multiplied and all that you have is
> multiplied, then your heart be lifted up, and you
> forget the Lord your God, who brought you out
> of the land of Egypt, out of the house of slavery,
> who led you through the great and terrifying
> wilderness, with its fiery serpents and scorpions
> and thirsty ground where there was no water,
> who brought you water out of the flinty rock,
> who fed you in the wilderness with manna that
> your fathers did not know, *that he might humble
> you and test you, to do you good in the end.* (vv.
> 1–16 ESV, emphasis added)

From this passage we can see that God allows Israel to be tested in the wilderness to accomplish something good, which includes Israel obtaining a discerning heart and discipline (vv. 16, 2, and 5 respectively). God, no doubt, allows us to be tempted for the same reasons. But in other cases, if truth be told, we simply do not know why.

However tantalizing the two preliminary questions I have posed might be, and however helpful the answers to them might be, it may come as a surprise to hear me say that they do almost nothing to prepare us for the main question of this essay: why did God allow Satan to tempt Jesus?

If you think about it for a minute, you will realize that God's reasons for allowing Israel to be tempted did not apply to Jesus. Unlike ancient Israel or us today, Jesus did not need to be deprived of food and later reprovisioned in order to remember God. Could Jesus ever forget God? No; he *was* God. Besides, according to Matthew's account of Jesus' temptation, God did not reprovision Jesus with manna; that was Satan's idea, which Jesus, for a reason to be discussed later, declined. Jesus was also unlike ancient Israel and contemporary believers in that he did not need to be humbled or to have the contents of his heart exposed as an aid to obeying the commandments of God.[2]

To answer our central question, we would do well to set aside any idea that God was primarily making Jesus an example for us or Israel to follow. Instead, we shall find it helpful to consider what the Gospel of Matthew understands the identity and mission of Jesus to be. We will do this by exploring two things: 1) what Matthew has been saying about the identity of Jesus so far in this Gospel and 2) whether there might be some overlooked clues in the story of Jesus' temptation that pertain to his mission and that, in turn, suggest why God would allow Jesus to endure these temptations.

What Has Matthew's Gospel Been Saying about Jesus Thus Far?

Chapters 1–3 provide context that is useful in addressing our big question and appreciating its relevance to us. From its beginning, Matthew's Gospel has been telling us that Jesus is the ultimate fulfillment of Old Testament prophecy.

Consider the following. In chapter 1, the initial genealogy of Jesus identifies him as the "doubly seventh"[3] and thus absolutely perfect descendent of Abraham. In the first years of his life, this perfect son, who is also a son of David, already fulfills a multitude Old Testament prophecies: he is born of a virgin, he comes from Nazareth, he

2. Hebrews 5:8 does say that Jesus learned obedience through what he suffered, but presumably, he did not learn obedience in the same way as we, who by nature are prone to disobedience because of our sin, learn it.

3. Jesus emerges after three generations of fourteen individuals (i.e., six of seven), making the arrival of Jesus the climactic and preeminent seventh of seven generations.

is called out from Egypt as the new Israel, and so on. In chapter 2, the story of the magi who follow the star serves literally to "high light" the place of Jesus' birth as, in the prophet Isaiah's words, "a light for the Gentiles" (Isa 42:6; 49:6 NIV). Soon thereafter, in chapter 3, John the Baptist proclaims that an era of God will be unleashed upon the world when John's successor comes. Since John the Baptist is described as an Elijah figure, it is hardly surprising to find that his successor, Jesus, is clearly portrayed as similar to Elijah's successor, Elisha. As Elisha had twice the endowment of the Spirit that Elijah had (2 Kgs 2:9), so Jesus is John's superior. Like Elisha, Jesus performs astounding miracles, including feeding a multitude with a small portion of bread (Matt 14:13–21; 15:32–39; cf. 2 Kgs 4:42–44) and bringing the dead back to life (Matt 9:18–26; cf. 2 Kgs 4:32–37, 8:1–5; 13:20–21). The ministry of Jesus, the new Elisha, supersedes that of both Elijah and John. In the story of Jesus' baptism that follows John's proclamation in chapter 3, he passes through the waters in a manner akin not only to that of both Elisha and Elijah, but also to that of Joshua and Moses. Finally, immediately prior to the temptation narrative, God himself pronounces his favor upon Jesus with the words "This is my beloved Son, with whom I am well pleased" (3:17 NRSV). The declaration that he is God's son ties him to David, and the Lord being well pleased ties Jesus also to the suffering servant of Isaiah. In the end, we are left wondering which positive figure in the Old Testament Jesus does *not* fulfill.

My point is this: the Gospel of Matthew is telling us that Jesus has embodied important prophets, the Messiah, and the suffering servant of Isaiah and is the climactic fulfillment of the Old Testament. This leads us to recognize, by the time we come to chapter 4, that God is doing something prophetically climactic in and through Jesus that is about to change the course of world history.

If you are or have spent any time around a parent, or if you have owned a puppy, you know what it means to have a sixth sense that detects when the child or puppy is doing something in the background that is not normal and is potentially dangerous. You know that if you do not immediately intervene, something you do not like is going to happen. It must have felt like that to Satan. He likely sensed that God was up to something big that was going to prove disastrous for him. So, Satan decided that he would try to nip this in the bud. He would deal with Jesus in the best way he knew how: as his tempter.

In light of our survey, we can surmise that the temptation of Jesus was more than a redemption of Israel's failures against temptation on its desert journey. Jesus had come as the divinely favored embodiment of Israel's prophetic heritage, poised to inaugurate God's promised era of deliverance. The contest between Jesus and Satan was a high-stakes cosmic battle. But our background portrait of Jesus' identity only further raises the question: why did God allow—or, as we shall see, actually arrange for—Satan to tempt Jesus?

Four Overlooked Clues That Help Unlock the Mystery

The first clue comes at the beginning of the narrative: Satan is awarded the opportunity to tempt Jesus. Verse 1 reads, "Then, Jesus was transported by the Spirit into the desert to be tempted by the devil" (my translation). Typically, the beginning of the verse is translated "Jesus was led by the Spirit," which could easily be taken to mean that Jesus spiritually discerned that he should go into the desert. But that is not what the text says. It makes clear that Jesus was actually "taken up"—as in hauled or transported—by the Spirit into the desert. And why? As the text also makes clear, for the purpose of being tempted by Satan.

What could be odder than this? We know the story so well that we might overlook the apparent incongruity of God's decision with the larger narrative of redemption. God bringing Jesus to the desert to be tempted by Satan makes about as much sense as the unthinkable scenario of King George VI of England, in the middle of the Second World War, transporting Winston Churchill to Adolf Hitler's home and leaving him there for over a month. Why would the Spirit of God do that to Jesus? Being righteous, holy, and good, God must have had a reason. This reason, which has thus far eluded us, will be the answer to our main question.

The second odd clue in our story is that there is an unstated assumption that Jesus must not invoke his supernatural powers during his temptation. Why not? Surely there could be nothing inherently wrong with the divine Son of God performing a modest miracle for the sake of his own provision, especially since, according to Deuteronomy 8:3, quoted above, God was happy miraculously to provide Israel with bread-like manna after they were tested in the desert by a lack of food. Why could Jesus not provide the same for himself? We are not told, but there must have been a reason.

My point in presenting the first and second clues is that something extraordinary is going on that is unique to Jesus' identity and mission but that remains difficult to understand. Whatever the reason, the Spirit of God must have had a purpose for handing Jesus over to Satan for temptation. And whatever the reason, Satan seems to have understood that the rules of engagement for Jesus included the prohibition of the use of supernatural powers. Otherwise, Satan would not have tempted Jesus to invoke them. What reason could there be?

The third and fourth clues are not so much odd as often overlooked. Together they clinch our understanding as to why God allowed Satan to tempt Jesus. Both remaining clues come from the second temptation, which, according to Matthew, goes like this: "Then the devil took him into the holy city and set him upon the pinnacle of the temple and said to him, 'Since you are the Son of God, throw yourself down'" (v. 5, my translation). After this, Satan offers testimony from Scripture (Ps 91:11–12) that God's angels will intervene and protect him from harm (Matt 4:6). Jesus then tells Satan that Scripture also declares that one should not put God to the test (4:7).

The third clue relates to the place from which Jesus is tempted to come down: it is high up on a pinnacle at a place where sacrifices are made. Note that there is another point in Jesus' ministry in which he is perched high up in a location where sacrifice is being made: when he is lifted up on a cross. The fourth clue is that the exact same words Satan uses to taunt Jesus to come down from the pinnacle of the temple appear later in Jesus' ministry on the lips of those who tempt him to come down from the cross. I am referring to Matthew 27:39–44, which reads:

> And those who passed by derided him, wagging their heads and saying, "You who would destroy the temple and rebuild it in three days, save yourself! *If you are the Son of God, come down from the cross.*" So also the chief priests, with the scribes and elders, mocked him, saying, "He saved others; he cannot save himself. He is the

> King of Israel; *let him come down now from the*
> *cross,* and we will believe in him. He trusts in
> God; *let God deliver him now, if he desires him.*
> *For he said, 'I am the Son of God.'"* And the rob-
> bers who were crucified with him also reviled
> him in the same way. (ESV, emphasis added)

Here we finally understand what is happening. Satan's temptation of Jesus to come down from the height of the temple complex, including the words he uses, are a dress rehearsal for a time later in Jesus' ministry when he will be tempted with those same words to come down from the cross and by so doing, as in the earlier temptation, prove the favor of God and his status as God's Son.

We have found the answer to our question. Why did God allow Satan to tempt Jesus? In order to prepare Jesus for his suffering and death—a suffering that, to be success-ful, required of Jesus, as in his temptation, that he not use his supernatural powers to help himself.

So, what can we learn from this remarkable event?

First, the devil—whether trying to trip up Jesus or us—is no match for God. While trying his best to destroy the purposes of God, Satan was all the while helping to fulfill them. We would do well to remember from the ap-parent logical inconsistency of the Spirit of God mandat-ing that Jesus be tempted by Satan that God has a reason for what he does, whether we know it or not. Occasions like this, when we can say, "Aha, now I understand," ought to give us comfort and hope for the times when we remain in the dark as to why God would permit—or even, as here, arrange for—something that seems harmful and that makes no sense to us.

Were God later to have left a phone message for Satan, he perhaps would have said something like this: "Hello, Satan, it's God here. I could not be happier with the results of your attempt to thwart my purposes; without knowing it, you helped prepare my Son to endure the cross so he could procure the salvation of the world. Farewell, unwitting coach!" The irony and shock for Satan are laughable.

But we should not entirely make light of this. After all, Satan is altogether bad news, dangerous, and capable of causing great harm, especially if we succumb to his temptations. For good reason our Lord taught us to pray, "Lead us not into temptation, / but deliver us from [the] evil [one]" (Matt 6:13 ESV). But let us have no doubt about this, and take great comfort from it: the devil is in a novice league compared to God. There is no contest: Satan is an eternal loser, whereas God always ultimately prevails. Two things the apostle Paul wrote underscore this:

> We know that all things work together for good for those who love God, who are called according to his purpose. (Rom 8:28 NRSV)

> No temptation has overtaken you that is not common to man. God is faithful, and he will not let you be tempted beyond your ability, but with the temptation he will also provide the way of escape, that you may be able to endure it. (1 Cor 10:13 ESV)

Second, so hard was it for Jesus, as the Son of God, to endure suffering and death that God ordained that Jesus attend boot camp to prepare for it. It is hard to imagine anything so difficult that Jesus would have to train for it. But the cross, so our text implies, was such an occasion. And what more ruthless and challenging boot-camp sergeant could there be than Satan? Our text, in effect, tells us that Jesus underwent rigorous training in enemy territory, under the most ruthless general in the land, and fought with live ammunition.

Consider what added torment Jesus must have experienced from knowing about the suffering that lay ahead for him and having the power immediately to stop it. Our Lord's agony in the garden and his statement to the disciple who drew his sword, "Do you think that I cannot appeal to my Father, and he will at once send me more than twelve legions of angels?" (Matt 26:53 ESV), are but faint glimpses into the divine mystery of untold agony, endured for us. The chorus of a hymn puts the matter simply and well: "He could have called 10,000 angels, but he died alone for you and me."

Knowing that God used Satan to prepare Jesus for the agony and humiliation of the cross teaches us much about the wisdom of God, the folly of Satan, and the magnitude of difficulty that Jesus faced in dying on the cross for our sins.[4]

Scripture: Matt 4:1–11.

Questions:

1. In what ways does the fact that Jesus had to experience temptations in preparation for his death compel you to appreciate him and the gospel more?

4. The reader may be curious about the role the first and third temptations play in relation to the explanation of Jesus' temptation here offered. I suggest that Jesus' first temptation, involving hunger (and presumably thirst), finds an echo in the offering to Jesus, and his refusal, of wine mixed with gall (Matt 27:34). Similarly, Jesus' third temptation, involving the offering to him of the kingdoms of the world, was something Jesus was here given practice at resisting until *after* his suffering and death, when, also on a mountain, *God* gave him authority on heaven and earth (Matt 28:18; cf. Dan 7:14, 27.).

2. Do you agree that knowing that God had a purpose for Jesus' temptations can be a source of help and comfort when we face hardship for reasons we do not understand? And if so, what inexplicable hardships have you faced that you might now be better able to deal with?

3. Seeing how God here completely outwitted Satan, in what ways do we overestimate Satan's power? In what ways do we need to be mindful of his power and remain vigilant? What is the right balance?

3

Called by the Light of the World

Judy Paulsen

In her book *Teaching a Stone to Talk*, Annie Dillard writes the following:

> On the whole, I do not find Christians, outside of the catacombs, sufficiently sensible of conditions. Does anyone have the foggiest idea what sort of power we so blithely invoke? Or, as I suspect, does no one believe a word of it? The churches are children playing on the floor with their chemistry sets, mixing up a batch of TNT to kill a Sunday morning. It is madness to wear ladies' straw hats and velvet hats to church; we should all be wearing crash helmets. Ushers should issue life preservers and signal flares; they should lash us to our pews. For the sleeping god may wake someday and take offense, or the waking god may draw us out to where we can never return.[1]

---

1. Dillard, *Teaching a Stone to Talk*, 40–41.

As Dillard points out, it is a problem when Christians forget or, as philosopher William Placher suggests, "domesticate" the transcendence of God.[2]

This is one of the reasons why we need Scripture. Scripture gives us both God's immanence and his transcendence. In fact, Scripture often veers wildly and disconcertingly from one to the other. Matthew 4 is a prime example. This chapter includes the mysterious words of Isaiah that a "great light" is seen by people sitting in darkness and in the shadow of death (Matt 4:16). Light, suddenly breaking into the muck and misery of the world, gives hope where there was no hope. This chapter also includes Jesus' own mysterious proclamation—in the Greek, it typically means "heralding"—that the kingdom of heaven, that is, God's kingdom, has come near and that the people need to "repent," a word that literally means to turn. Imagine having to do a quick U-turn toward something for which you have always longed but were afraid was only a dream. That beautiful, powerful, glorious reality, the kingdom of God, has now finally come near!

Indeed, Matt 4 gives us a tantalizing glimpse of God's transcendence. The King of heaven and his kingdom have now come near. As fragile, mortal creatures, we cannot fully know all that this means. On the one hand, Dillard is right. God's transcendence, in light of Matt 4, should inspire awe and maybe even terror. On the other hand, we know that this transcendence, power, and otherness belong to the one we most desire to know. So yes, this Gospel passage speaks powerfully of the transcendence of God. But then there is a disconcerting shift as it moves suddenly back and forth between the mysterious and the seemingly mundane, telling of a recently relocated rabbi

2. Placher, *Domestication of Transcendence*, 7.

who, perhaps not coincidently, is also related to a man recently arrested by the Romans. The rabbi leaves Jerusalem and heads north to Galilee, traveling unremarkable roads to the unremarkable towns of Nazareth and, eventually, Capernaum. This travelogue is followed in the text by the rabbi walking along the shore of the lake, calling out to two sets of brothers who are laboring at their trade as fishermen. The rabbi tells them to come and be his disciples. The invitation is not elaborate. He says to them simply, "Follow me" (4:19 NRSV). Here is where the narrative gets interesting again: the brothers do choose to follow this man. They leave their nets, their boat, their livelihood, and even their father. These four fishermen drop everything to follow the call of this Jesus. Anyone who has also heard this call understands what is happening. The light of the world has come calling. The text does not explain it. It simply describes it.

Throughout the New Testament, we see other people *suddenly* doing strange things as a result of this person Jesus. A tax collector walks away from a guaranteed income. A woman makes a spectacle of herself at a dinner party. A madman camping out among tombs is suddenly in his right mind. Four friends cut a hole through someone's ceiling. A little girl, whose death is already being mourned, sits up and eats some lunch. A thief, *while being crucified*, asks to be remembered. A prominent religious leader lovingly wraps the corpse of a man deemed to be a religious heretic. A scholar of the Jewish law begins to preach the very message he previously abhorred.

Why do they do these things? It seems to be because in Jesus they encounter someone unlike anyone else. As surely as the whole of Scripture shows us glimpses of God's transcendence and immanence, somehow, in this person

Jesus, that transcendence and immanence perfectly come together and then meet these men and women.

Further, this passage teaches *how* Jesus meets and calls these fishermen brothers. First, it says that Jesus *sees them*. He sees them in the midst of their very ordinary lives, in which they might not be expecting much of anything. Perhaps their hope is simply to earn enough to pay the rent, make ends meet, and, if they are lucky, enjoy a little extra on the side. Jesus, however, sees something else for them, and because of how he sees them, the significance of their lives will be forever changed. Second, Jesus *speaks to them*. "Follow me. Come along. I am going to make something different out of your lives" It is less of an invitation than a commandeering. Finally, Jesus *gives them a promise* attached to that commandeering: "I'm going to make you fish for people" (v. 19, adapted from NRSV). This promise seems to be at the very heart of, the very point of, his calling them.

This passage demonstrates why disciple-making is not just one of many things that the church is to do. Rather, disciple-making is to be at the very heart of the church's purpose. "Follow me, and I will make you fish for people" (v. 19 NRSV).

Andrew, Peter, James, and John could not have anticipated all that would come as a result of their response on that fateful day. They could not see that their "fishing" would result in an amazing catch that would extend for two millennia. The catch was and is so great because the fish that they caught, in turn, became fishermen. Their being sent out with the message of the light of the world started something that has rippled across the ages: from the first apprentices of Jesus gathering in the temple courts in Jerusalem to groups of Hellenistic Christians meeting in homes along trade routes of the Greco-Roman world; from entire Germanic tribes being baptized in European rivers to Celtic monks setting off for distant coasts in their hide-covered currachs; from Jesuits arriving in snowy Huron villages on Turtle Island to Victorian men and women setting out on steamships bound for India, China, Japan, and the continent of Africa; and from today's "reverse" missionaries coming to the West from China, Nigeria, and Guyana to the most recent new millennial apprentices of Jesus learning to follow their Lord. The great movement known as Christianity seems to have started with those words recorded in Matthew's Gospel account: "Follow me, and I will make you fish for people."

But that is not the full picture, is it? Christianity and its transmission across the ages and around the globe began not as a result of these words but as a result of people encountering Jesus and being shaped by him. The disciples first thought of him as Jesus of Nazareth, but they eventually came to know him as Jesus the Christ, their Lord and Savior. Just two decades later, here is how these early followers were describing this Jesus who had called them:

> He is the image of the invisible God, the first-born of all creation. For by him all things were created, in heaven and on earth, visible and invisible, whether thrones or dominions or rulers or authorities—all things were created through him and for him. And he is before all things, and in him all things hold together. And he is the head of the body, the church. He is the beginning, the firstborn from the dead, that in everything he might be preeminent. For in him all the fullness of God was pleased to dwell, and through him to reconcile to himself all things, whether on earth or in heaven, making peace by the blood of his cross. (Col 1:15–20 ESV)

That description, taken from Paul's letter to the Colossians, is the sort of thing that comes out of people who are encountered by Jesus, the light of the world, who is also the man from Nazareth. He is the message we bear.

May we never forget that Jesus has commandeered us to *share* the good news of his kingdom, which is come and is coming, so that those who still sit in darkness (Matt 4:16) may meet and be changed by Him.

Scripture: Matt 4:12–23.

Questions:

1. Have you experienced a call to follow Jesus? Share with your small group, or record in a journal, what this looked like in your own life.

2. What amazes you the most about Jesus? What most puzzles you?

3. Can you think of a situation in which you shared your faith with someone? Have you thought about that as "fishing for people?" Why or why not?

4

The Grace of Nakedness

Ephraim Radner

This meditation is not an exposition of the Beatitudes. Rather, it simply claims that the Beatitudes are Jesus' declaration to the "crowds"—to us—about who we are, fundamentally. More specifically, the Beatitudes are about the basis for our *Christian* identity being just the lives that God has given us—all of us, anybody—as a gift. Christian identity is not about what we do with our lives, not about our character, not about any "value added." Christian identity is just the lives themselves. Everything flows from that. Christians are not special human beings they just know what a human being is. Moreover, a human being is naked from God.

Of course, nakedness can be viewed as a bad thing. "Left naked," we say with sadness about someone reduced to wretchedness or abject failure. The famous Italian philosopher Giorgio Agamben has used the image of nakedness to describe how modern states strip individuals of their substantive meaning as citizens with agency and character, consigning these individuals to the realm of "bare life" at the mercy of sovereign states or corporations:

refugees, insurance claimants, prison inmates, medical clients—they are all gears in an educational or economic system that grants or removes certification and benefits in ways that far outstrip the individual's democratic agency. The naked either survive or die. And even if one does survive, bare survival itself has neither dignity nor worth.[1]

Is this right? Is nakedness a reduction to mere "survival"? Maybe. The coats of skin that God gives Adam and Eve to cover their nakedness as they are driven from the garden is a small gesture allowing them to escape that ultimate reduction (Gen 3:21).

However, reduction is just one version of nakedness. There is a deeper sense in which nakedness, as a fundamentally Christian term, is not a reduction at all, politically or morally. Nakedness is not a state a person enters when bad things take place—divine judgment or social oppression. Nakedness is simply who we are. Nakedness is, in fact, deeply revelatory of the mystery of human beings in the first place. In the early modern period, small Christian sects of so-called Adamites appeared in Bohemia and England, practicing the joyful nudity of our first ancestors. Why not? Nakedness, after all, is good: it is the glimmering light that marks the miraculous act of the God "who brings into existence things that do not exist" (Rom 4:17; my translation).

A few years ago, not long after my wife and I moved to Toronto, my father, who was in his early eighties, had a stroke. He is an internationally respected applied mathematician—my father is a smart man—and at that time he lived in Washington, D.C., and was still working full-time as an academic. I immediately drove down and met my

1. Cf. Giorgio Agamben, *Homo Sacer: Sovereign Power and Bare Life* (Stanford, CA: Stanford University Press, 1998).

stepmother, and together we went to the hospital. Initially, he was not doing well; his heart had been deeply compromised. He could not talk and could barely move about. I spent the next few days there with him, and I watched as the nurses helped him, changed him, got him to the bathroom. Many years had passed since I had seen my father naked. Now, unlike Noah's sons, it was my duty to see him stripped. Here he was, shriveled, brittle, helpless, the shell of an old insect of some kind—the man who conceived me, raised me, protected me, gave of himself to me, loved me, the one against whom I had struggled so long in many ways, as sons do with strong fathers. My father was listless skin and bones. Nevertheless, his own self—his "real" self, you could say—was still bound up here. It was astonishing. At one point, the cardiologist came in to explain what had happened and what they were going to do about his heart. My father weakly motioned for a pen and then tremulously wrote something on a napkin. At first we could not understand what he had written—lines, some numbers, Greek letters. Then the doctor's face brightened up: "Yes," he said, "your equation exactly describes what the medicine will do." My father wanly nodded and tried to smile.

I have never seen a clearer conjunction of a creative mind and spirit with the earthly, fragile, transitory body of this life—a conjunction that is proclamatory of something marvelously deep, miraculous, and true, as Job says: "Naked I came from my mother's womb, and naked shall I return" (Job 1:21 ESV; see also Eccl 5:5). In this famous verse, Job adds, with a resounding exclamation of praise, a kind of "therefore": "Blessed be the name of the Lord!" The result is praise, which is of the nature of this conjunction. You could call this a gospel of sorts.

What I have offered so far is a long introduction to the Beatitudes of Matt 5. It is, however, important because we need to separate the Beatitudes from the common approaches to interpreting them. Over the centuries, the Beatitudes have often been read in one of two ways. The first treats the Beatitudes as a guide to morals. With this interpretive approach, Christians have read the text ascetically; "Blessed [or "happy"] are the poor in spirit" (Matt 5:3 ESV) means "Be humble, learn meekness, fast, be peaceable, repent with tears, and suffer for your faith." The second way, which has become more common recently, reads the Beatitudes, if not ascetically, then politically: "Blessed are the poor, for God cares for them, especially along with the pacifists, the powerless, the oppressed, and the marginalized." To be sure, both concerns, the aesthetic and the political, are not wrong. However, I doubt that we should understand the Beatitudes as if Jesus is standing before the crowds, and us, laying out a *program* of life, a set of marching orders. More fundamentally, Jesus is simply declaring a divine reality. He is not saying that human insistence on power, money, or prosperity is a vice. It may be that, but simply to make such an observation is to neglect the true problem: the human insistence on these things is simply *untrue*. Jesus is not saying that such insistences are unjust, though they can be. The point is that they are *unreal*. Thus, Jesus' judgment on the contradiction of the Beatitudes is not so much condemnation as astonished pity: "Fool!" Jesus says to those who have denied this truth and reality. "Fool! For tonight your soul is required of you" (Luke 12:20; my translation)—that is, you have forgotten who you are!

Indeed, the Beatitudes are true simply because this is who the one true human being *is*. As the famous Latin

translation of Pilate's presentation of Jesus to the crowds—
to us—has it: *Ecce Homo!* "Behold the Man!" (John 19:5
NASB). The Beatitudes make little sense unless we realize
that these kinds of teachings are first of all about Jesus as
just this man. Writers like Gregory of Nyssa insisted on
this. Jesus is the poor one, the one who was rich and became poor for us, not counting divinity as "something to
be grasped" (Phil 2:6 NASB); Jesus is the thirsty one, who
cried out from the cross, "I thirst" (John 19:28 ESV); Jesus is the meek one, the one upon whom the Lord laid the
transgressions of us all and who did not lift up his voice
(Isa 53:6–7); Jesus is the peacemaker who traveled around
preaching peace to people far and near (Isa 57:19; Eph 2:17)
and who is himself our peace, breaking down the wall of
hostility between people (Eph 2:14); and Jesus is the one
who blesses his enemies: "Father, forgive them; for they
know not what they do" (Luke 23:34 KJV). The Beatitudes
are enacted by Jesus; therefore, they are his gospel. But most
importantly, Jesus, the man upon whom all human beings
gaze, lifted up before the eyes of the world, is the man who
is stripped bare and hangs naked on the cross.

The nakedness of Jesus is a central claim of the gospel. It has been resisted in many ways over the centuries,
but has generally been asserted from the days of the early
church. When artists began making images of the cross
and deposition, they depicted a cloth over Jesus' groin,
for modesty's sake. Few, however, doubted the assumption
that since his clothes were distributed among soliders at
his bloodied feet, he, like all Roman criminals, was left
hanging above them utterly denuded. Only once he was
dead did they take him down and wrap him up again like
someone in a hospital bed. "Truly this man was the Son
of God!" the centurion exclaims, looking upon this naked

body (Mark 15:39 ESV; also Matt 27:54). Naked, Jesus died. And naked he also rose (Luke 24:12), as the disciples discovered at his tomb, rifling through the scattered linens left behind.

In this way, God himself has shown us what is of true value—our very lives as his gift, its generosity ungrasped. Jesus is the Naked One, from birth to death to resurrection. Jesus is the one who is wholly *from* God (John 5:30). He did not make himself, but was sent; Jesus is also the one who is wholly *toward* God, who does not latch onto a life that is finally to be commended to the Father (e.g., Luke 23:46; John 13:1). In short, Jesus is sent from God and is going to God. Accordingly, we follow such a truth made manifest. We are poor, for we own nothing except what God has given us, and this too is what God will take from us at our deaths; we are meek, for there is no power that is intrinsically ours; we make peace, for the insistence on having our way is but a passing resistance to a journey that we cannot control; and we weep, for weeping is the inevitable result of recognizing our embedded powerlessness apart from God's gift. Blessed are those who are all and only God's, both from and to him, and not their own. Christians—followers of and believers in Jesus—are naked in just this sense. So we too proclaim, "The Lord gave, and the Lord hath taken away; blessed be the name of the Lord! (Job 1:21 KJV).

Nakedness in the Scriptures is not an ill. Oh, if only we could understand this! To be sure, in the garden, upon the opening of eyes that see how good and evil vie with one another, nakedness is fearful. To embrace the truth of who we are, in a world where suddenly we are tempted to see alternatives to the God who made us, is to shiver, to tremble, to run away, and to hide lest we be given over to the hands of something less good, less sure, less holy than the one who gave us breath. Nakedness as vulnerability is the product of knowing good and evil. However, there is no such thing as vulnerability when there is only God in view. Remember that! So, Adam and Eve enjoyed their nakedness until their God became obscured. They enjoyed, purely and solely, the fact that God had made them. Nakedness in the sight of God is the pure fulfillment of human life.

There is no vulnerability when we stand alone before God alone, nor is there any failure. We need to remember this as well in a world that both threatens us and leaves us battered in the face of unceasing judgments about our worth. In the recent movie *The Hidden Life*, Franz Jägerstätter, an Austrian farmer, is executed by the Nazis at the end of the Second World War because he refuses to sign an oath of allegiance to Hitler. Jägerstätter was a Christian, and the story is true. At one point, one of his interrogators says to him, "Why do you bother refusing to sign? . . . You'll make no difference to this war. Serving Christ? To what end? Two thousand years of failure."[2] From one perspective, yes, the whole Christian enterprise seems to be a "failure." Jesus' life did not amount to much; he could claim a few healings and followers—there were others like him in this regard—and he died in his early thirties. By these metrics, he was a failure like most people. But he was a *truly naked* man. He was a—the—perfect man. And there is no failure for such a one, because God has made him. *God.* The Alpha and the Omega. Furthermore, God *re*-made him too, nakedness being but the mark of that

2. These are paraphrases of the screenplay of *A Hidden Life* Directed by Terrence Malick. Fox Searchlight Pictures, 2019. pp. 78 and 32 available at https://www.simplyscripts.com/2019/11/19/a-hidden-life-for-your-consideration/ (accessed 3.16.21).

miraculous touch, the conjunction of dust and spirit, that is the Lord's own hand at work. That nakedness is you and I in our perfection—though we are not perfect yet, but only following after that perfection (Phil 3:12)—regardless of how those purported alternatives to God may try to assert or exploit our apparent vulnerability and failure. Franz Jägerstätter died a naked man. However, he was not reduced, but, rather, elevated. Nakedness, being without shame and thus invulnerable and without failure, is intrinsically elevating. Remember that too.

Notice that as Jesus goes to his death, Mark says, "And there followed him a certain young man, having a linen cloth cast about his naked body; and the young men laid hold on him: And he left the linen cloth, and fled from them naked" (Mark 14:51–52 KJV). In a way, the young man who fled naked—Mark himself, perhaps—was the first disciple of a new age! Similarly, when the resurrected Jesus encounters Peter by the lake, Peter stands there naked to his Lord's new gaze (John 21:7). Anything good starts with nakedness, for it is God's will that he clothes us with his own divine nakedness, his own perfection (2 Cor 5:3).

Blessed are the poor in spirit and in body; blessed are those who weep; blessed are the meek, the hungry, the thirsty, the open-handed, the empty-handed, the eager, the expectant, the followers, the one-step-after-anothers, the waiting, the from-God and the to-God, the all-gift; blessed is the bare life that neither the civil state nor a physical stroke can wipe away; blessed is the glorious life; and blessed is the life that says, in naked coming and in naked going, "Blessed be the name of the Lord," who is the "all in all" (1 Cor 15:28).

Scripture: Matt 5:1–2

Questions:

1. Why do we think nakedness is a bad thing?

2. What does God's creation of human beings as naked yet not ashamed tell us?

3. Are the kinds of people presented by the Beatitudes meant to be imitated?

4. What does the nakedness of Jesus—in birth, death, and resurrection—tell us about ourselves?

5. Why does Job praise God's name in Job 1:21?

5

Jesus Makes Us Salt and Light

ANN JERVIS

JESUS HAS ESCAPED THE crowds. As celebrities then and now have discovered, fame has its problems. Jesus has become so famous for his healings and preaching that he cannot go anywhere without being surrounded by vast crowds. Consequently, seeing the masses, Jesus went up a mountain (Matt 5:1).

According to the Gospel of Matthew, Jesus sits down on the mountain, and his disciples come to him (5:1). He then begins to teach what has come to be called the Sermon on the Mount (Matt 5–7). At the end of the sermon, Matthew writes that the crowds are astonished at the authority of Jesus' teaching (7:28–29), showing that people have caught up to Jesus even on top of this mountain. In the Sermon on the Mount, we are hearing words directed to Jesus' disciples while the crowds overhear.

What I will discuss in this essay appears in Matthew 5 right after the Beatitudes. In all of the Beatitudes except the last one, Jesus has addressed his hearers indirectly: "Blessed are those who are poor in spirit," "Blessed are those who experience sorrow" (vv. 3–4, my translation), and so on. Only in the last beatitude does Jesus use personal pronouns: "Blessed are *you* when people insult *you* and harass *you* and speak all kinds of bad and false things about *you*, all because of *me*" (v. 11, my translation, emphasis added). In the following section, Jesus begins with the plural pronoun "you." "You are the salt of the earth". "You are the light of the world" (v. 13–14 NIV). Jesus has turned directly to his disciples, and he tells them who they are.

It might not be hard for his disciples to believe this about themselves. After all, they are in the inner circle of one of the most famous teachers and healers in Israel. "You are the salt of the earth and the light of the world." The disciples might easily understand Jesus to be giving them the same identity and commission that God has given to Israel—to be a light to the nations (Isa 42:6; 49:6), to be the people who preserve the earth. For men who have been far from the center of power in Judaism's religious and political life, this must be a heady idea.

Jesus, however, does not just tell his disciples the great news that they are important and crucial to the world, although he does tell them that. Jesus also informs them of their responsibility to be who they are. Jesus urges, even warns, his disciples to act in accordance with the identity that he has given them. Their identity means there is work to do—what Jesus calls "good works," deeds that the law and the prophets have prescribed. The disciples' identity is at once a call to action, a call to act in accordance with the commands of the law in a way that exceeds even the elite law followers, the scribes and the Pharisees.

If I were one of the disciples, Jesus' words would have thrilled and also terrified me. I might have felt that it was amazing to be given such a high calling—the kind of calling that God gave to Israel's founding father, Abraham. But I might also have felt scared about whether I could, or even wanted to, live such a rigorous life, a life of exceeding righteousness, a life of doing good works in such a way that people would know to glorify God because of what I was doing. That seems like a great deal to ask of a simple person.

Hold on: I am one of Jesus' disciples, and you are too. Jesus' words are addressed not just to his first disciples, but to all his disciples: they are words to you; they are words to me.

How do Jesus' words strike you? Do you feel up to—or even want—the task that Jesus demands, that is, to be the world's salt and light by doing good works and by fulfilling the law and the prophets?

I will not ask you to share your answer with anyone else. But as the one posing the question, it seems right that I should share mine. My answer is "No." No, I do not feel up to that task. But neither do I want to run away from it. Let me ponder that last thought first.

I do not want to run away from the crucial call of God to be the world's salt and light, not only because I want to be part of the kingdom of heaven—Jesus says, "Unless your righteousness exceeds that of the scribes and Pharisees, you will never enter the kingdom of heaven" (5:20)—but because I cannot see any other way ahead for the world.

You and I have given our attention to this book in part because we care deeply about God's world and because we are distressed about its political, social, and ecological mess. Whether or not we have put it to ourselves this way, we are here because we want to be salt and light for God's world. This is a daunting desire, not just because of the magnitude of the world's problems but, speaking for myself, because of my sense of smallness, irrelevance, and ineptitude. No, I do not feel up to the task that Jesus assigns his disciples, particularly if Jesus is asking me to help the world by being exceedingly righteous and doing good works in such a way that people glorify God rather than thinking that I am a good person.

Matters get even worse. Further on in the Sermon on the Mount, Jesus says, "You will be perfect like your heavenly Father is perfect" (5:48, my translation) Am I—are we—supposed to be like Jesus? The only perfect one, the only one whose righteousness exceeded that of the scribes and Pharisees? The one whose good works revealed God's glory? The one who is the light and life of the world?

After I take a deep breath, I back up and notice that Jesus is demanding such high standards of *his disciples*. He is not asking me—or any of us—to live with exceeding righteousness, to live perfectly, through our own willpower. He is not asking us to act out such righteousness with any natural capacities that we have for justice and love. He is asking us to do good works and fulfill the law *as his disciples*. He is asking us to behave righteously because he has made us able. By being near to Jesus, by being called by Jesus, we are given a new identity: salt and light for the world. We act out of who Jesus has made us to be.

The world's salt and light is not something that we can make ourselves into; it is something that God, through Jesus, has declared that we are. And this truth is our starting point for our actions in behalf of the world. It is not we ourselves who do good deeds. No, we do good works because God has made us the world's preservers and light-bearers; we do them as the salt and light that God has made us into.

Longstanding theological discussions circle around the concepts that Matthew presents here in Jesus' words: Do we do good in order to be saved, or because we are saved? Do we do good because we are naturally able to do so, or because we are made capable of doing so by God? Matthew does not offer direct answers to these theological—and pastoral and personal—questions. But Matthew does strongly suggest that Jesus' disciples can do good only because of his authoritative declaration. Jesus gives strong warnings about the importance of acting righteously; as noted already, their righteousness must exceed the scribes' and the Pharisees' righteousness. However, the overriding claim Jesus makes is that his disciples can be assured that they will enter that kingdom. Why? Because they are gathered around him. In the prayer that Jesus teaches later in his sermon, Jesus tells his disciples that they can share in his own relationship with God—"Our Father who art in heaven" (Matt 6:9 RSV). They can expect that their sins will be forgiven if they forgive others (v. 12); they can ask to be steered away from temptation and delivered from evil (v. 13).

In other words, Jesus welcomes those around him into own his relationship with God and, by extension, into the assurance that, as he says in the first Beatitude, theirs is the kingdom of heaven (5:3). Those whose poverty of spirit has driven them to seek the healing and life that Jesus offers—theirs is the kingdom of heaven.

Jesus' teaching is meant to help them, and us, understand how to act in the world, not so that we can be saved but because we are saved. Jesus wants us, those who gather around him, to know that we have a critical role to fulfill for the sake of God's world. Jesus is the one who has made us able to fulfill that role. The basis for our good works is who we are. Moreover, recognizing who we are involves seeing the one who has made us who we are, seeing Jesus.

Jesus, the one who gives the Sermon on the Mount, is the one Matthew will describe as dying because of our sins and being raised to display his power over that death. The preacher on the mountain is also the healer, the one who heals the infirmities that prevent good works, the one who heals us of our sins. Jesus is the one who gave himself to us in order to reveal the powerlessness of sin and the power of good.

When I recognize who is speaking, I hear Jesus' call for righteousness not as a demand but as a gift. "When," as the old hymn says, "I survey the wondrous cross," which looms large even while Jesus is the sought-after celebrity on the mountain, I realize Jesus' and God's costly gift. More specifically, I am reminded that our good works are made possible because God chose to make us able—at the cost of his own Son's betrayal and suffering and crucifixion.

When I meditate on who is preaching the Sermon on the Mount—not a demanding judge, but the one who died for us—then I am drawn away from judging my abilities to do good and from focusing on whether or not I have lived up to Jesus' demands. Instead, I experience simple, humble gratitude that comes from understanding that God has inexplicably made all of us who gather around Jesus able to do God's will.

Reminding ourselves and each other of this—that Jesus' life, death, and resurrection are the only reason we can do good works—is critical. If we forget this fact, we risk losing our identity. If we fail to reshape our self-understanding on the basis of Jesus' declaration of who we are, we may be people who work hard to bring justice and do good, and we may even achieve some glory for our good works, but we are not the world's salt and light.

We ourselves may not be able to see the difference in outcomes between doing good out of our own resources and doing good as Jesus' disciples, but this is not ours to know anyway. We are only asked to be with Jesus and hear him tell us who we are, encouraging us to do good works for the sake of God's world. We can do that right now in focusing our attention on this book, and we do this when we gather around Jesus in communion, taking his body and blood, given for us the night he was handed over for our sins, given for us so that we can be the world's salt and light.

We are asked to see again the great gift God has given us in Jesus: we are enabled to act as Jesus, the light and life of the world.

Scripture: Matt 5:13–20

Questions:

1. What do you think of as your identity? If you think of it as the world's salt and light, how will this affect your actions?

2. What does righteousness mean to you?

6

Choose Life

CATHERINE SIDER-HAMILTON

I AM NOT SURE that there is such a thing as a typical childhood. If there is, mine was not it.

For instance, my dad had a wily sense of humor. When my brothers and I were little, loud, and rambunctious, we spent a lot of time right before dinner on our stomachs in the back yard with dad, looking for four-leaf clovers. Four-leaf clovers do exist, but their frequency is something like one in ten thousand. My dad searched diligently in the grass before dinner, and we searched with him. To this day I feel certain that I will find one in that backyard if I just look long enough.

How do *you* say the counting-off rhyme, "Eeney, meeney, miney, moe?" It has tigers in it, right? "Catch a tiger by the toe." Not in my childhood. This is how my dad taught us to say it:

Eeney, meeney, miney, moe
Catch a *Trojan* by the toe.

Since our lives were already full of Greek gods, Trojan horses, Cyclops, and Sirens, this being my dad's choice of bedtime story, "Trojan" never struck me as strange. For years we three kids went around happily catching Trojans instead of tigers, until one day someone said, "What?" Then I realized that Trojans were not as ubiquitous as I had thought.

Here is yet another example. We never heard anyone swear. My parents never swore. My aunts and uncles never swore. My grandparents and all my older cousins never swore. "Oh, bother!"—that was Mom's expletive of choice. Since we also had no television and did not go to the movies much, it was a long time before I became acquainted with swearing.

My parents did not swear—either profanely, to punctuate their sentences, or in God's name, to give weight to their word—for the simple reason that the Bible says you should not swear. My parents, their parents, and all my uncles, aunts, and cousins took the Bible seriously, more or less.

On this point they were not simplistic. They were thoughtful people. My Brethren in Christ (BIC) grandfather, who was a pastor, quoted Tertullian in his sermons and had Martin Luther's *Commentary on Galatians* on his shelves; my father went on to write a book on Tertullian and became a professor of classics; one of my uncles is a professor of church history; a cousin is a professor of Old Testament. They were not simplistic. They were thoroughgoing. They believed that if they were to call themselves Christian, then they should follow Jesus Christ.

And Jesus said you shall not swear.

> You have heard that it was said to those of old, "You shall not swear falsely, but shall perform your oaths to the Lord." But I say to you, do not swear at all: neither by heaven, for it is God's

> throne; nor by the earth, for it is His footstool
> . . . Let your "Yes" be "Yes," and your "No," "No."
> (Matt 5:33–35, 37 NKJV)[1]

In this small commitment to not swearing (something Christians now almost universally ignore), in this small act of taking Christ seriously as Christians, they heard the rest of what Jesus says to us in this passage of the Sermon on the Mount. They heard the "why" as well as the "what." Do not swear. Why? Because you are not the one who has the power to swear. Because you cannot, by swearing, turn one hair of your head white or black.

Swearing is a category mistake. To swear is to mix yourself up with God. Do not swear by heaven, because heaven is not yours; it is the throne of God. Do not swear by earth because the earth is not yours to bend to your will either.

> Then the Lord answered Job out of the whirlwind: . . .
> "Where were you when I laid the foundation of the earth?
> . . . Who laid its cornerstone
> when the morning stars sang together
> and all the heavenly beings shouted for joy? (Job 38:1, 4, 6–7)
>
> Do you give the horse its might?
> Do you clothe its neck with mane?
> Do you make it leap like the locust?
> Its majestic snorting is terrible." (Job 39:19–20)

Do not swear by heaven or earth, because their creatures are not the creatures of your hand. The earth is not yours to do your bidding or to stand surety for your vow. "The earth is the Lord's and all that is in it" (Ps 24:1).

1. Unless otherwise noted, all Scripture quotations in this chapter are from the NRSV.

Not to swear is an act of obeisance to God. Not to
swear is to call him Lord and King. It is to cede all authority in heaven and on earth to him. Not to swear is to say
that he is our God and "we are his people, and the sheep of
his pasture" (Ps 100:3). Therefore, we live not by the word
of our mouths, but by His word.

"By God, you will pay for this," we might say. But no.
This is not what Jesus calls us to say, even in our heart of
hearts. Jesus calls us to remember the words of the apostle
Paul, which draw on Deuteronomy 32:55, "Vengeance is
mine, I will repay, says the Lord" (Rom 12:19). And even
worse, in some ways, is to use the name of Jesus as an
expletive or simply an expression of surprise. To use the
name of Jesus or of God simply as an exclamation mark,
so that it no longer has any reference to Jesus himself, is
to erase our Lord from our lips and from our lives. It is to
use his name for our own purposes—not to invoke him as
Lord, but simply to give our words power.

Jesus calls us to recognize the radical lordship of God
in heaven, on earth, and in his holy temple, neither to erase
our Lord nor to take his lordship for ourselves. Swearing
gets the whole world backwards. It asks God to follow our
will; it sets us up in the place of God. On the contrary, we
are asked to follow God's will. That is where our blessing
lies—not in *our* way, not in *our* words, but in his.

We are called to bend the knee. We are called to bend
the knee before the great King of all the earth and to wear
this worship so completely that it becomes ingrained, our
second skin. We are to wear this worship so completely
that we do not swear casually. Indeed, we cannot, because
we hear in his name the Lord of heaven and earth. Not to
swear at all is to practice bending the knee, to name God
Lord, every day.

There is another concern to consider too. From the view of child, such as me or either of my siblings in years past, the tongue that does not swear is sweet. There is a gentleness in it. To a child who is not used to it, the swearing tongue strikes the ear with a peculiar violence. Letting your "yes" be "yes" and your "no," "no" involves peaceable language, and this language looks to the peaceable kingdom. In this simplicity of speech, our tongues and our words strive even here, even now, for that time when God will be all in all.

The same concern for truth and peace underlies all the other commandments that Jesus gives us in the Sermon on the Mount. Do not bring an offering for God to the altar on a Sunday if you know that your brother has something against you. Do not come to church and say "peace" until you have made peace with him. Let it go deep, the peace that you say; let it be true. Pursue the difficult reconciliation. It is God's peace that we practice here. Jesus has died for it. To live truly, deeply, radically in peace with each other is to call Jesus Lord. Anything less is to deny him. To take God's word seriously, to live it wholly—word by word, friend by friend, day by day—is to call Jesus Lord. This is our worship.

It is also our joy. Moses says to Israel, "I have set before you life and death, blessings and curses. Choose life" (Deut 30:19). God asks us to take his word seriously so that we might have life, so that we might discover what it means in our marriages to love long and steadily and with a whole heart, so that we might discover the comfort waiting for us at the end of a long love. God asks us to take his word seriously so that we might learn what it means in our homes and church communities to walk together with each other through difficult reconciliation into peace, so that we might learn, in every word we say, what it means to worship God day by day, what it means to wear Christ as a second skin, even on our lips.

"Choose life," Moses says to Israel. "Choose life," Jesus says to us today. "You shall love the Lord your God with all your heart, and with all your soul, and with all your mind, and with all your strength" (Mark 12:30). Love him and obey him and worship him with every word you say. *This is life for you.*

Scripture: Matt 5:21–37; Deut 30:15–20; 1 Cor 3:1–9

Questions:

1. How does it both comfort you and challenge you to know that the words that you say, even causally, can be an act of worship for God, the one who is the great King of all the earth and who sent his Son to die for you?

2. In what ways have you experienced the life and the love described in this sermon through the small act of using your words as worship?

7

Are You Faking Your Religion?

PETER MASON

ASH WEDNESDAY IS AN invitation to observe a holy Lent by self-examination, penitence, prayer, fasting, charitable giving, and meditation on the word of God.

Reading and Meditating on the Word

Lent invites us to read the story, to soak up the word. To exalt the Bible is not to encourage the sin of bibliolatry, nor is it to replace Almighty God. Rather, it is to declare that the God we worship is present at all times, in every place, and in each circumstance. At creation, God spoke. In forming a people, God called Abraham. In self-revelation, God spoke through Moses, establishing how God should be known, followed, worshipped, and obeyed. In rebuke tempered with mercy. In Jesus, the Word made flesh. In a story of love, forgiveness, victory, and promise.

Movies will sometimes have a scene in which someone receives a letter from a faraway friend or lover. The recipient opens the letter and begins reading silently. The camera zooms in over his or her shoulder, and the audience can see the text. Soft music plays, with the voice of the sender overtop, and the reader hears the content of the letter. These scenes give an illustration of what it is like to meditate on the Bible, hearing the very voice of God. This kind of reading, to be sure, does not take place upon the reader's first encounter with the text. What comes first is the careful, close, unromantic studying and deciphering of the text, with the aid of a dictionary or perhaps a friend. In this kind of study, it is essential to pay close attention to the language, consult commentaries, and deal with texts in a critical way. Then, after this "academic" encounter, comes the second kind, the reading-as-hearing encounter. The transition from the first to the second is the transition from mere reading to meditating, hearing the Bible as God's word given to us, which Lent encourages.

There is a danger of neglecting either kind of interaction with the text. All critical study conducted in an objective, arm's-length way leads to cynicism, unbelief, and even despair. But just as problematically, an exclusively subjective, self-centered, fundamentalist attitude leads to a stubbornness that insists, "This is what the Bible means to me regardless of the wisdom of tradition and scholarship and the experience of the church down the ages." To meditate on the word of God is, therefore, both to get as clear an understanding of the text as possible and to enter into its message as the hearer, the recipient, to find yourself in God's story as a participant in his redemptive action.

As an exercise, choose a biblical text as the basis for reading and meditating. This could be an epistle from the New Testament, a section of a Gospel, a portion of Old Testament history, or an utterance from the prophets. Whatever your choice, let it first address you and then your circle of companions, your church, and eventually your community. Ask in silence, "Speak, Lord; I want to listen." A good place to start would be the Beatitudes (Matt 5:3 12).

Self-examination

In one sense we are constantly carrying out a process of self-examination. Almost unconsciously we are asking and answering the question "How am I doing?" We glance in a mirror, and we routinely replay past conversations or encounters with one another. We look for signs of approval, and we fear signs of failure.

However, the kind of self-examination that Lent promotes is more complex and nuanced. It is said that the unexamined life is not worth living. Self-examination should be deliberate, regular, and connected to some external criteria. We should ask ourselves regularly, "How am I doing in relation to a set of rules, a mentor I admire, or the qualities and behaviors of my peers?"

Think a little further about the term "self-examination." Does it refer to me examining myself, or am I the self that is to be examined, perhaps by someone else or by some mechanism? Think of a medical examination. There are certain basic self-examination functions, such as poking, prodding, and flexing. The danger is that you may either overestimate or underestimate the state of your own health. On the one hand, you may rationalize away a serious problem; on the other hand, you may imagine yourself to be at death's door when in fact you are in no serious danger. So, naturally, you supplement or even correct your own diagnosis with the aid of the medical profession.

What, then, are the diagnostic tools that Lent presumes? Briefly, there are three. First, there is Scripture, which contains the true story of God's self-revelation, including God's sovereign purposes for all creation. There is, therefore, an obvious link between reading and meditating on God's word on the one hand and self-examination on the other. The possibilities and options for using Scripture in self-examination are endless. The Christian could use, for example, the Ten Commandments, the prudential morality of Proverbs, the life and teaching of Jesus, the domestic codes of Colossians and Ephesians, the works of the flesh and fruit of the Spirit listed in Galatians 5, and the qualifications for church leadership in the Pastoral Epistles. Above all, we should desire God to be our examiner in the spirit of Psalm 139:23–24 and plead, "Search me, O God, and know my heart; / test me and know my thoughts; / See if there is any wicked way in me, / and lead me in the way everlasting" (NRSV).

Second, there is liturgy. Think of the promises that are made at baptism and confirmation. These can be found in *The Book of Alternative Services* of the Anglican Church of Canada and usefully read annually in Lent.[1]

Third, there is the input of another person whom you regard as a trusted confidant. A spouse, partner, or close friend may serve this function, but there are pitfalls. He or she may gloss over your failures or, conversely, point out only your faults. It is, therefore, important to seek out an appropriate partner in the dialogue of self-examination. There should not be an obvious imbalance of power in such a relationship. After all, we are equals in pursuing the holiness that is pleasing to God. This process is about discerning the will of God with the guidance of a wise person. Remember: although Lenten self-examination may appear overwhelmingly negative, there is always a need for some

1. *Book of Alternative Services*, 154, 625.

affirmation. Lent is eventually followed by the grace expressed on Good Friday and then by the victory celebrated on Easter Sunday.

Penitence and Repentance

There is a logical progression from reading and meditating on God's word to engaging in self-examination. The word lays out the nature and purposes of God in relation to his creation, particularly with respect to our place in it as his human creatures. That word establishes God's expectations and norms for our relationship to him. In turn, we are challenged to examine the degree to which we live up to those divine standards. When that self-examination makes clear that we are, by nature, in an impaired relationship with God, we are bidden to take the humbling steps of throwing ourselves upon the mercy and grace of God offered through the Savior Jesus Christ.

Too often, self-examination can mislead us into denial. "If we say we have no sin, we deceive ourselves, and the truth is not in us" (1 John 1:8 NRSV). We are bidden to confess our sins, counting on God's forgiveness and cleansing. That confession is preceded by penitence, which is a deep feeling of remorse, of genuine sorrow, sadness, and embarrassment for what we have done. The liturgy of confession gives us words to capture a true spirit of repentance. Note, however, that this language of confession has softened over the years. For instance, the prayer of confession from the 1918 Canadian *Book of Common Prayer* is as follows:

> *Minister.* God spake these words and said; I am the Lord thy God Thou shalt have none other gods but me.

People. Lord have mercy upon us and incline our hearts to keep this law.

Minister. Thou shalt not make to thyself any graven image, nor the likeness of any thing that is in heaven above, or in the earth beneath, or in the water under the earth. Thou shalt not bow down to them nor worship them: for I the Lord thy God am a jealous God and visit the sins of the fathers upon the children unto the third and fourth generation of them that hate me; and show mercy unto thousands in them that love me and keep my commandments.

People. Lord have mercy upon us, and incline our hearts to keep this law.

Minister. Thou shalt not take the Name of the Lord thy God in vain: for the Lord will not hold him guiltless, that taketh his Name in vain.

People. Lord have mercy upon us, and incline our hearts to keep this law.

Minister. Remember that thou keep holy the Sabbath-day. Six days shalt thou labour, and do all that thou hast to do; but the seventh day is the Sabbath of the Lord thy God. In it thou shalt do no manner of work; thou, and thy son, and thy daughter, thy man-servant, and thy maid-servant, thy cattle, and the stranger that is within thy gates. For in six days the Lord made heaven, and earth, the sea, and all that in them is, and rested the seventh day: wherefore the Lord blessed the seventh day, and hallowed it.

People. Lord, have mercy upon us, and incline our hearts to keep this law.

Minister. Honour thy father and thy mother; that thy days may be long in the land which the Lord thy God giveth thee.

People. Lord, have mercy upon us, and incline our hearts to keep this law.

Minister. Thou shalt do no murder.

People. Lord, have mercy upon us, and incline our hearts to keep this law.

Minister. Thou shalt not commit adultery.

People. Lord, have mercy upon us, and incline our hearts to keep this law.

Minister. Thou shalt not steal.

People. Lord, have mercy upon us, and incline our hearts to keep this law.

Minister. Thou shalt not bear false witness against thy neighbour.

People. Lord, have mercy upon us, and incline our hearts to keep this law.

Minister. Thou shalt not covet thy neighbour's house, thou shalt not covet thy neighbour's wife, nor his servant, nor his maid, nor his ox, nor his ass, nor any thing that is his.

People. Lord, have mercy upon us, and write all these thy laws in our hearts, we beseech thee.

The prayer of confession quoted above may seem over the top. Consequently, the confession in the contemporary *Book of Alternative Services* has been toned down considerably:

we confess that we have sinned against you
in thought, word, and deed,
by what we have done,
and by what we have left undone.
We have not loved you with our whole heart;
we have not loved our neighbours as ourselves.
We are truly sorry and we humbly repent.
For the sake of your Son Jesus Christ,
have mercy on us and forgive us,
that we may delight in your will,
and walk in your ways,
to the glory of your name. Amen.

In short, penitence means acknowledging and accepting my share of the world's evil, suffering, and sin. Sometimes we are the sinners; other times we may be the ones "sinned against." However, penitence must include or lead to repentance. As James 1:22–25 instructs:

> Do not merely listen to the word, and so deceive yourselves. Do what it says. Anyone who listens to the word but does not do what it says is like someone who looks at his face in a mirror and, after looking at himself, goes away and immediately forgets what he looks like. But whoever looks intently into the perfect law that gives freedom, and continues in it—not forgetting what they have heard, but doing it—they will be blessed in what they do. (NRSV)

Similarly, John the Baptist heralded Jesus' ministry by preaching a baptism of repentance. When asked what that meant, he replied, "Bear fruit in keeping with repentance. Share your extra coat and your food with someone in need; do not collect more taxes than permitted; do not extort the poor and innocent" (paraphrase of extracts from Luke 3:8, 11, 13–14). Saint Paul, summarizing his ministry before King Agrippa, says, "I declared that both Jews and Gentiles should repent and turn to God and do deeds consistent with repentance" (paraphrased from Acts 20:21).

Both Scripture and Anglican liturgies make it evident that sins come in two broad categories: sins of commission and sins of omission. The General Confession of the 1962 Canadian *Book of the Common Prayer* says:

> Almighty and most merciful Father, We have erred and strayed from thy ways like lost sheep, We have followed too much the devices and desires of our own hearts, We have offended against thy holy laws, We have left undone those things which we ought to have done, And we have done those things which we ought not to have done; And there is no health in us. But thou, O Lord, have mercy upon us, miserable offenders. Spare thou them, O God, which confess their faults. Restore thou them that are penitent; According to thy promises declared unto mankind in Christ Jesu our Lord. And grant, O most merciful Father, for his sake, That we may hereafter live a godly, righteous, and sober life, To the glory of thy holy Name. Amen.

As to sins of omission, the parable of the talents (Matt 25:14–30) stresses the sin of sloth or mediocrity. We must not peg ourselves permanently as one of the slaves. Rather, we should move from one to three to five talents depending on the circumstances. In the parable of the good Samaritan (Luke 10:25–37), the omitted sin is that of indifference, which essentially says, "That is not my responsibility," or, "I am retired." Finally, remember that self-examination, penitence, and repentance lead to grace and forgiveness.

Fake Religion

When Jesus says, "Beware," as he does in Matthew 6:1 (NRSV), he tells us to be careful, to take heed, and to listen up. We need to pay attention, for there is danger ahead. In this passage the danger is not atheism, secularism, violence, or high crimes and misdemeanors. The danger is fake religion or distorted religion. Jesus, therefore, reserves some of his harshest criticisms and attacks for those religious leaders who practice religious customs with ulterior motives.

In Matthew 6, he does not name these leaders, but by the end of his ministry, he calls them out by name or position (Matt 23:1–7). The label he brands them with is "hypocrite." The word refers to an actor in a play, that is, someone who acts out a role or who pretends outwardly to be what he or she is not inwardly. Not all Pharisees were completely bad. One suspects that many Pharisees began their service with appropriate motives and intentions but that over time they succumbed to the temptations of power and prestige. We must not be too quick to side with Jesus and assume that we are not among those whom he rebukes. On the contrary, this text is for you and me to reflect on.

Here in Matthew 6:1–18, Jesus identifies three typical Jewish religious duties and practices. They are not controversial, and they are not exclusive. Rather, they are merely examples of worshipping God and serving others.

The real issue is motivation and the demand for openness, transparency, and consistency. There is always potential for a reward behind the scenes. If I fulfill my religious duties with an eye to other people recognizing and praising me, then I will get that reward. But it is a shallow, superficial, fleeting reward, especially in comparison to the reward of God's approval encompassed in the phrase,

"Well done, good and faithful servant" (Matt 25:23 NIV). Such a reward is not earned, not to be coveted; it is nothing more or less than a surprising, unexpected, divine bonus. It is an assurance of God's grace to us.

So, this text focuses on three acts of devotion: giving, or charitable donations; praying; and fasting. Each of them, and others like them, can either express our love of God and our neighbors or become vehicles of our own self-promotion.

1. Charitable donations: Jesus warns against giving to God's work in order to satisfy our own ego. There is a passage where Jesus and his disciples are in the temple, watching some people showing off with big gifts. In this passage, a poor widow gives a few coins, which is all that she has, and is commended by Jesus. He says, "Truly I tell you, this poor widow has put more into the treasury than all the others. They all gave out of their wealth; but she, out of her poverty, put in everything—all she had to live on" (Mark 12:41 NIV)

2. Praying: Praying, for the Jews of Jesus' day, was not controversial or exceptional, as should be the case for us today. It is what we do. This warning is not against public temple or church worship. It is rather about a kind of informal or impromptu prayer that contains an element of showing off, making an impression of super-spirituality. You know it when you see it; others know it when you do it. Beware!

3. Fasting: It is evident from the text that fasting—depriving oneself of some necessity for a period of time—was an accepted practice. In our day, we too may choose to give up some activity or substance to remind ourselves that we are dependent on God and not on anything

else and that we should not be addicted to any worldly pleasure. However, unlike the Pharisees in our text, we are to fast in secret, where nobody else will see and admire us. Accordingly, we must not boast about our spiritual self-control and superiority.

Earth to Earth, Ashes to Ashes, Dust to Dust

Earth, ashes, and dust are the primordial elements of the universe. God made Adam out of dust. We are mortal. We do not live forever in an earthly state. We shall turn to ashes, then to dust, all of us in our common humanity. Dust was the source of our common origin, and it is our common earthly destiny. Therefore, on Ash Wednesday, we must receive the mark of ashes, remembering our frail, broken humanity while clinging to the promise of Easter, which will come forty days afterward, "in sure and certain hope of the resurrection to eternal life through our Lord Jesus Christ."

In the spirit of doing your religious exercises in secret, think about how long and under what circumstance you will keep the ashes on your forehead. Wipe them off before too long. Do not go out into the crowds saying, "Look at how spiritual I am!" But perhaps keep them on long enough so you can look at them in a mirror by yourself. Then only you and God will see the real and true you.

Scripture: Matt 6:1–6, 16–21.

Questions:

1. How might a recent reflection upon the word of God be leading you toward repentance?

2. What are some other motivations that have been influencing your acts of devotion toward God? Take some time to surrender these to God and be once again moved that the grace of Jesus Christ covers even our impure motives.

8

Be Clean

STEPHEN ANDREWS

When Jesus came down from the mountain great crowds followed him. And now a leper approached him, bowed before
him, and said, "Sir, if only you will, you can make me clean."
Jesus stretched out his hand and touched him, saying, "I will;
be clean." And his leprosy was cured immediately.

(MATT 8:1–3 REB)

GOOD MORNING. WELCOME TO *Sine Nomine* Church, lo-
cated on the beautiful shores of Lake Souci, in the thriving
metropolis of Beaucoup de Soucis, Ontario. If you are a
newcomer, then please raise your hand, and one of our
greeters will bring you a complimentary set of envelopes.
We hope you will stay for coffee—and perhaps a meeting—after the service.

Sermons are often improved through the use of illus-
trations, so I have asked one of my good friends and fellow

parishioners if he might help me this morning. I am going to ask Truman if he would mind stepping out from the choir and present himself at the top of the chancel steps. Truman is a little embarrassed to do this, but he does it anyway. This is one of the things I really like about Truman. He is a humble fellow at heart and a little shy, but he would not risk embarrassing the bishop by refusing to do what he asks!

So, here is Truman, smiling nervously and looking at the floor. Now, I want to present him to you as a prime example of a "good Christian." I think you would all agree with me in this assessment. After all, what could any of you say that is critical of Truman? He is an honest fellow. His values are noble. He is a family man who is devoted to his wife and children. He has the occasional drink, but he is never given to excess. He obeys the law and has a good reputation in the community. And although I would not tell you the amount of his weekly giving, I can say that he is very charitable. He has a positive outlook on life. He plays his part in the work of the church, as you can see by the fact that I had to call him out of the choir. So, who would disagree with me that if anyone deserves to be called a "good Christian," it is Truman and people like him? Goodness, I can even see his wife and kids nodding in agreement! If that is not proof, then nothing is!

I rather admire Truman's life, which is, in fact, an improvement of my own. He knows this too, I suspect, by the way he is smiling just now. Well, I am afraid that it is time for him to wipe that silly grin off his face because if the truth be known, he is not all that great as a Christian. It is not that I am trying to be rude or humiliate him. Indeed, compared to my own life, as I said, his seems quite impressive. But unfortunately for him, God does not use me or anybody else in this congregation as a standard by which to measure his life. God's criterion is the standard of Jesus Christ, and when evaluated against Jesus, even Truman's life does not appear to be so impressive.

For instance, Truman was overheard this week saying some things about another person that were not very complimentary. The comments were, in fact, rather unkind and critical, and they served no constructive purpose. It makes me wonder whether or not he had considered Jesus' question, "Why do you see the speck in your neighbor's eye, but do not notice the log in your own eye?" (Matt 7:3 NRSV). Then there was that situation at work when Truman told his colleague that he did not have the time to follow up on a particular matter, when in reality he has been trying to avoid dealing with this issue for weeks. He might have remembered Jesus' warning, "Plain 'Yes' or 'No' is all you need to say; anything beyond that comes from the evil one" (Matt 5:37 REB). Finally, I noticed on my way into church this morning that Truman seemed a little chippy toward the choir director. Such an attitude certainly does not cohere with Jesus' instruction that "if you remember that your brother or sister has something against you, leave your gift there before the altar and go; first be reconciled to your brother or sister, and then come and offer your gift" (Matt 5:23–24 NRSV).

You may take your place in the choir again, Truman. I am sorry to have paraded your shortcomings before the whole congregation. People will undoubtedly have pity on you and tell me after the service that I have been too hard on you. However, I doubt that is any consolation, and I would not blame you if you left quietly by the side door and never came back to church!

Nevertheless, I am reluctant to apologize, for two reasons. The first is that we need to be reminded that no one is a "good Christian" because no one is really "good." Jesus himself said so to the rich young ruler: "Why do you call me good?" he asked, "No one is good except God alone" (Mark 10:18 ESV). Moreover, if God is our measure, then complete goodness is unattainable. As Jesus said in his Sermon on the Mount, "Be perfect, therefore, as your heavenly Father is perfect" (Matt 5:48 NRSV). God's standards for us are high, impossibly high. This is why, as much as preachers emphasize the importance of reading Scripture for comfort and instruction, there ought to be a label attached to every Bible, saying, "Warning: This book contains language that some may find offensive. Reader discretion is advised."

The second reason I am hesitant to apologize is this: in all likelihood, the person in our midst who is right now closest to real faith, closest to finding healing and forgiveness, and closest to being touched by God is none other than Truman himself. This is because the result of Truman's public shame is that now, more than ever, he knows what it is like to be a leper. And as we see in Matthew 8:1–4, the glory of the gospel is that Jesus heals lepers.

There are at least two aspects of the life of a leper in the ancient world that are relevant to us today. In the first place, leprosy in the Bible is not always what we call leprosy today, which is more technically known as Hansen's disease. Leprosy in the Bible can be any one of a number of disfiguring and sometimes painful skin diseases. With as many as seventy-two classifications created by the scribes, leprosy was a common disease in Palestine and was the subject of superstition and fear. It was often understood as a sign of God's judgment on the sufferer.

Second, it is important to know that the ancient Jews had strict regulations regarding the treatment of lepers, which are laid down in the legal code of Leviticus 13–14. There it is said that a leper must wear clothes that are torn, that his hair is to be unkempt and dishevelled, and that he is not allowed to dwell within the city walls. In an effort to contain the disease, the leper was required to live alone; when he saw anyone approaching, he was compelled to cover his upper lip and shout, "Unclean! Unclean!" Similarly, other Jews were not allowed to come near a leper, for fear that they would become ritually contaminated. Moreover, it says something about the status of the leper in the ancient world that the only thing *more* polluting to a Jew was a dead body.[1] To have leprosy was to serve a sentence. Other illnesses needed to be healed; lepers needed to be cleansed.

When we understand the isolation and ostracism, the dejection and self-loathing, that lepers experienced, our attention is arrested by two unusual things in Matthew 8:1–4. The first thing is the faith of the leper. The fact that he even approaches Jesus is remarkable, as it is a bold violation of law and custom. The story teaches us that even law and custom cannot be allowed to prevent people from coming to Jesus. Moreover, the way he addresses our Lord provides an important lesson in faith. "If only you will," he said to Jesus, "you can make me clean" (8:2 REB). Here we have a petition that is both reverent and certain. There is nothing presumptuous or demanding. There is no pleading or cajoling. There is no doubt. There is only a humble expression of deference ("if only you will") and a bold statement of trust ("you can make me clean"). Proper faith has these two components: it is confident in the power of God, and it is respectful of the will of God.

1. E.g., Josephus, *Antiquities of the Jews* 3.264.

Second, it is extraordinary that Jesus responds to this man's faith by touching him. Jesus could keep his distance and heal the man, as he does with the centurion's servant in Matthew's next story. Despite religious restrictions and social taboos, and despite the risk of being ostracized himself, Jesus reaches out freely and with compassion, saying, "I will; be clean" (v. 3 REB). At that moment, the leper feels a sensation that he has missed during the whole time of his illness: the touch of another human being. And in that touch, in this scandalous engagement, we are witnesses to a contest between corruption and wholeness, and the unclean becomes clean. Jesus is not polluted by the leper's disease; rather, the leper is cleansed by Jesus' contagious holiness. Incidentally, one historical consequence of this story is that Christianity is the only world religion that has always made a place for lepers.

Now, whom is this story intended to benefit today? My hope is that it will be a source of inspiration and encouragement to Truman and to everyone like him. I think this is Matthew's intent in telling the story.

Those who have been reading through the Gospel of Matthew while using this book will know that the healing of the leper is the first event to be related after Jesus' Sermon on the Mount (chs. 5–7). The purpose of the opening illustration with Truman was to create the kind of space that we would all be in if we had just finished a careful and soul-searching reading this sermon. For it is difficult to hear Jesus' words without feeling, in the end, dispirited, defiled, and hopelessly inadequate. We fall shamefully short of the beautiful characteristics he describes, lacking humility, forgiveness, self-control, faithfulness, generosity, patience, and trust; we fall shamefully short of the example of his own life. That is to say, the sensitive reader of Saint

Matthew's Gospel can by this point feel very much like a leper who is not fit to come into the presence of God.

And yet, herein is the gospel: in our isolation and impurity, in our infirmity and imperfection, Jesus wills to touch us and cleanse us. We do not enter into his presence; he enters into ours. The story of the cleansing of the leper is but a figure of the incarnation. This was not missed by the church's early preachers, who noted that the incident takes place when Jesus descends from a mountain, before taking up the company of a leper. John Chrysostom comments, "The Lord therefore comes down from heaven, as from a high mountain, to cleanse the leprosy of our sins"[2]

In the end, I hope Truman did not slink out of the side door in disgrace. I hope he realized that he is not alone in this leper colony that we call the church. For I, leper that I am, dwell with him. And what binds us together is our faith-full petition, "Sir, if only you will, you can make me clean." For then we shall see that we are joined by Another, who shall touch us in love and grace and proclaim, "I will; be clean." Amen.

Scripture: Matt 8:1–4.

Questions:

1. When was the last time that you, like the leper in Matthew 8:1–3, felt utterly helpless and undeserving of God's attention? What did you experience from this situation?

2. Why is it so critical for Christians to remember the hopeless and sinful state that they are in apart from the grace of Jesus Christ?

2. John Chrysostom, *Opus Imperfectum* 6.23 (p. 95).

3. What are some practical ways of cultivating the faith and humble heart of a leper?

9

Watch and Be Ready

THOMAS POWER

IT MAY HAVE ESCAPED your notice, but the *Oxford English Dictionary* has recently added hundreds of new words to its stock. Among those added, I was curious about the word "becket." I thought it might have something to do with the celebrated murder, in the year 1170, of Archbishop of Canterbury Thomas à Becket at the hands of knights encouraged by Becket's rival, King Henry II. To my dismay I discovered that the new word "becket" had nothing to do with death or killing but had a more prosaic meaning: a spade for digging turf! Nevertheless, as Archbishop Becket discovered, life has its uncertainties and surprises, but ironically, the one thing certain about life is death.

A desire for readiness in the face of death is one of the reasons why Christians have given Matthew 24:36–45 some attention, and clearly, being ready for death is something that is necessary for us all. However, the primary reason this passage has drawn attention is, of course, that it speaks about the second coming of Jesus. We have a natural curiosity about the end of the world and Jesus' second coming. But this passage cautions us against indulging that curiosity too much.

Society

Why is such caution necessary? I think it is because in our broader culture, speculation about the end of time causes people to gravitate to either of two extremes. On the one hand, there are those who think obsessively that the end is imminent. Given predictions about health crises, a climate disaster, international terrorism, dangerous technological innovation, and so on, it is understandable that people would feel that way. Whole sections of society have bought into the notion that we are living in the end times, and they indulge the idea excessively.

The other extreme, of course, concerns those who live in the here and now on the basis of "Eat, drink, and be merry, for tomorrow we die," with no care for the future and no sense of the eternal. This attitude has also seeped into our culture, and to no surprise, given its hedonism, rampant individualism, and practice of living in an eternal present with short-term stimuli and instant gratification. Just as obsession with the end is pervasive, so also is the denial of the end.

Christians

Christians, in their own way, are not immune to adopting opposite views on the subject of the end. Historically, there have been believers who have held that social activism and global mission, that is, human effort, can hasten the end of time and the second coming. Others, however, have held that the world is under the grip of evil and cannot be redeemed until Jesus returns again and inaugurates a new age.

But in the sections that precede and follow this passage in Matthew, Jesus warns against adopting either of these views—obsessive interest or apathetic denial—too readily, no matter how compelling the evidence. If neither of these extremes are options, what, then, are followers of Jesus to think? We are left with these verses, which instruct us on what attitude to have. What does Jesus teach us?

It is important to note that for Mathew's audience, the passage would have had a particular meaning. For those living in first-century Jerusalem, there is a prediction of some great crisis that is imminent. The disciples are curious and have two basic questions for Jesus: "When will this be, and what will be the sign of your coming and of the end of the age?" (24:3 NRSV). In answer, Jesus tells them, "Truly [or "amen"] I tell you, this generation will certainly not pass away until all these things have happened" (Matt 24:34 NIV). In essence, Jesus believes that these traumatic events will occur within the lifetime of his disciples. And we know that they were to culminate in the destruction of the temple in AD 70.

The disciples' questions about the return of Jesus are our questions also. And Jesus gives a clear answer: "Of that day and hour no one knows, not even the angels of heaven, nor the Son, but the Father alone" (24:36 NASB1995). And elsewhere he says, "It is not for you to know the times or dates the Father has set by his own authority" (Acts 1:7 NIV). Although Jesus is certain of his return, he does not claim to know the exact time when it will happen. Such knowledge is the Father's alone. Jesus is clear: his return is certain, and it will come, but he cannot offer specifics as to its timing. But Jesus does not leave us without guidance in the matter. Instead, he provides us with analogies that help us understand what attitude to have toward his return. These analogies tell us three things.

1. The Return of Jesus Will Be Sudden and Unexpected

We are told, "For the coming of the Son of Man will be just like the days of Noah. For as in those days before the flood they were eating and drinking, marrying and giving in marriage, until the day that Noah entered the ark, and they did not understand until the flood came and took them all away; so will the coming of the Son of Man be" (Matt 24:37–39 NASB1995).

The people of Noah's time were living their normal lives, too busy to think of anything beyond the immediate present. Then the flood came and swept them away. Three things about the story of Noah stand out:

A. It was sudden. There was no warning, and the people were caught off guard.

B. They were unprepared. People were living their ordinary, everyday lives. They had no idea of what was to come until it was too late.

C. The event was unknowable: "They did not *understand* until the flood came and took them all away" (24:39 NASB1995, emphasis added).

In citing Noah, Jesus wants us to know that his return will be as sudden and unexpected as the flood was. It will come just as people are doing their ordinary activities. It will come suddenly and unexpectedly.

2. The Return of Jesus Will Bring Separation

"Then there will be two men in the field; one will be taken and one will be left. Two women will be grinding at the mill; one will be taken and one will be left" (24:40–41 NASB1995). Again, as in the days of Noah, people will be engaged in normal activities, like working, when the day will suddenly arrive. Jesus states that there will be two men in the field and two women grinding meal. They will be busy with their daily tasks when Jesus arrives unexpectedly, and then it will be too late for them to prepare for his coming.

As well as repeating what the account of Noah conveyed—that is, the sudden and unexpected nature of Jesus' return—these verses emphasize that the return of Jesus will bring division and separation, whether in families or among fellow workers.

In each case, one person in the pair will be taken, and the other will be left. In other words, no matter how physically close two people may be on earth, there is no guarantee that they will have the same eternal fate. One may be rewarded, the other condemned. There will be a sharp division between outwardly similar people who are working together. There will be a division of humanity: some will be taken, some left behind.

This passage and others like it have been interpreted to imply that one person will be swept up by God in a miraculous act of rescue while the other person is abandoned. In reality, as the flood came and suddenly washed away those who did *not* believe Noah, so the return of Jesus will see the unbelieving swept away while believers remain. It is also important that an invading force in first-century Jerusalem would likely have taken away some people for certain death, leaving others as they were. Furthermore, in many places Jesus sees judgment as separation: those who are being judged or rejected are depicted as being excluded, cast out, or told to depart. What Jesus describes in Matthew 24 is not some rapture of the righteous, but the decisive sweeping away of the unrighteous at the return of Christ. Therefore, to be left at Jesus' second coming is to be assured of salvation. Being taken is judgment; being left is salvation.

So, Jesus instructs that his return will be sudden and unexpected and that when it comes, it will bring separation and division.

3. The Return of Jesus Requires Us to Watch and Be Ready

"Be sure of this, that if the head of the house had known at what time of the night the thief was coming, he would have been on the alert and would not have allowed his house to be broken into. For this reason you also must be ready; for the Son of Man is coming at an hour when you do not think He will" (24:43–44 NASB1995).

Here the householder represents any believer, and the thief who comes during the night represents Jesus. We know Jesus will come, but how can we plan for it? We should act as we do when we do not know the exact time of an important arrival: we should be alert and ready at all times, like a householder who waits and protects a home from robbers.

These few verses reiterate what has been said already: you do not know and cannot know when Jesus will return. But it also warns us that because of the sudden and unexpected nature of Jesus' return, and because of the separation that it will bring, it is essential to watch and be ready. Readiness should be the norm for believers because the time of Christ's coming is unknown. All you can do is be ready continuously. Keep watching, and be ready.

Readiness: Attitude

We now know that the return of Jesus will be sudden and unexpected, that it will bring separation, and that we need to be alert and ready. However, this passage is not just a prediction of the future. It is meant to impact attitudes in the present. What attitude of heart and mind should we have in light of Jesus' return?

Over twenty years ago, in January 1999, Israel's Ministry of Health announced plans to deal with what it termed "messianic madness" among the many thousands of Christian pilgrims who had arrived in the Holy Land for the end-of-the-millennium celebrations. It was predicted that about forty thousand of the anticipated 4.5 million visitors would need psychiatric help, with about one thousand requiring hospital treatment. Many of the visitors were expecting to witness apocalyptic events, including the return of Jesus on the Mount of Olives. The Israeli authorities also identified what they termed the "Jerusalem Syndrome," a condition afflicting apparently sane visitors who began to suffer from delusions that they were biblical figures involved in the end-times drama.[1]

This is not the kind of attitude that Jesus encourages by speaking of being ready for his return. Instead, what he calls us to do, and what this passage implicitly instructs us to do, is be faithful, trusting, and obedient.

1. S. Hunt, "Introduction: The Christian Millennium—an Enduring Theme," 1.

Faithfulness, Trust, and Obedience

The purpose of Matthew 24:36–45 is not to speculate about the details of how and when the second coming is to happen. In fact, one lesson to be learned from this passage is the absurdity of human speculation about the timing of the end. It is true that Scripture provides certain signs, but not for the purpose of making detailed, sequential predictions. Rather, the first purpose of the passage is to promote faith. If we had a specific outline of the future, that would be a hindrance, not a help, to faith.

This passage calls for trust on our part. We know that God brought about the fulfillment of Old Testament prophecies with the coming of Jesus. This fact calls us to trust the eternal word of God when it says that Jesus will come again. God fulfilled one set of prophecies with the sending of his Son. Accordingly, we trust, and we wait for the fulfillment of the texts assuring us of his second return.

Matthew 24 also calls for obedience. Jesus is clear: his return is certain, and it will come, but he does not offer specifics as to its timing. The matter is settled and final. Our response to Jesus' teaching should be obedience. It therefore follows that attempts to devise a prophetic or apocalyptic timetable, of which there have been many throughout history, or attempts to read the mind or plans of God are acts of disobedience. Such attempts ignore Jesus' clear teaching. Simply to accept what Jesus says about his return is an act of obedience.

Readiness: Practice

As stated above, since there is no way of knowing when the Son of Man will return, the only sensible thing to do is adopt a state of constant readiness. This readiness includes faith, trust, and obedience. But these three behaviors might seem too passive. What are we supposed to do while we wait for the second coming? How do we live day to day while we watch and stay ready for His return?

Readiness shown by faith, trust, and obedience requires being fully committed to God, Jesus, his kingdom, his good news, his worship, and his mission in the world. It means bringing God's transforming love into every part of our lives: our homes, the workplace, school, politics, and so on. It means serving God's purpose in the world and the needs of other people. While we wait in readiness for the Lord's return, and despite all the predictions of doom generated by the obsessions and denials of our culture, our duty is to proclaim the gospel to all humanity.

In the words of 1 Peter 4:7–10: "The end of all things is near; therefore, be of sound judgment and sober spirit for the purpose of prayer. Above all, keep fervent in your love for one another, because love covers a multitude of sins. Be hospitable to one another without complaint. As each one has received a special gift, employ it in serving one another as good stewards of the manifold grace of God" (NASB1995).

Paul, writing to the Thessalonians, says, "Now brothers and sisters, about times and dates, we do not need to write to you, for you know very well that the day of the Lord will come like a thief in the night . . . So, then, let us be alert and self-controlled . . . putting on faith and love as a breastplate, and the hope of salvation as a helmet" (1 Thess 5:1–8).

Yet, in all this we must keep in view that nothing we do or fail to do can hasten or delay the second coming of Jesus. That event is unknown and unknowable. It will happen in God's good time. The end will come only by divine intervention.

Scripture: Matt 24:36–45

Questions:

1. How is the flood of Noah like the second coming of Christ?

2. What is the one thing we can be certain of regarding the day and the hour of Christ's second coming?

3. What does it mean to be ready for Jesus' return if we do not know when he will come?

4. What practical steps can you take to be ready for the return of Jesus?

Bibliography

Agamben, Giorgio. *Homo Sacer: Sovereign Power and Bare Life* (Stanford, CA: Stanford University Press, 1998).

The Book of Alternative Services of the Anglican Church of Canada. Toronto: Anglican Book Centre, 1985. https://www.anglican.ca/wp-content/uploads/BAS.pdf.

Calvin, John. *Sermons on Galatians.* Translated by Kathy Childress. Edinburgh: Banner of Truth, 1997.

John Chrysostom. *Opus Imperfectum.* Translated by Jane Doe. Grand Rapids: Baker, 2010.

Dillard, Annie. *Teaching a Stone to Talk: Expeditions and Encounters.* New York: Harper & Row, 1982.

George, Timothy. *Theology of the Reformers.* Rev. ed. Nashville: Broadman & Holman, 2013.

A Hidden Life. Directed by Malick, Terrence. Fox Searchlight Pictures, 2019. (transcripts https://www.simplyscripts.com/2019/11/19/a-hidden-life-for-your-consideration)

Hunt, Stephen. "Introduction: The Christian Millennium—an Enduring Theme," In *Christian Millenarianism From the Early Church to Waco*, edited by Stephen Hunt, Bloomington & Indianoplis: Indiana University Press, 2001.

Kittelson, James M. *Luther the Reformer: The Story of the Man and His Career.* Minneapolis: Fortress Press, 1986, 2003.

Placher, William C. *The Domestication of Transcendence.* Louisville: Westminster John Knox, 1996.

www.ingramcontent.com/pod-product-compliance
Lightning Source LLC
Chambersburg PA
CBHW060423090426
42734CB00011B/2431